NIGHT TERRORS

NIGHT TERRORS

Sex, Dating, Puberty, and Other Alarming Things

ASHLEY CARDIFF

GOTHAM BOOKS

GOTHAM BOOKS
Published by the Penguin Group
Penguin Group (USA) Inc., 375 Hudson Street,
New York, New York 10014, USA

USA | Canada | UK | Ireland | Australia | New Zealand | India | South Africa | China

Penguin Books Ltd, Registered Offices: 80 Strand, London WC2R 0RL, England
For more information about the Penguin Group visit penguin.com.

LIBRARY OF CONGRESS CATALOGING-IN-PUBLICATION DATA

Cardiff, Ashley.
   Night terrors : sex, dating, puberty, and other alarming things /
Ashley Cardiff.
      pages cm
   ISBN 978-1-592-40786-6 (pbk.)
   1. Cardiff, Ashley. 2. Cardiff, Ashley—Childhood and youth. 3. Adolescence—
United States. 4. Teenagers—Sexual behavior—United States. 5. United States—
Social life and customs—21st century. I. Title.
   PS3603.A7348Z46 2013
   306.73092—dc23
   [B]   2012049013

Printed in the United States of America
10 9 8 7 6 5 4 3 2 1

Set in Bell MT
Designed by Spring Hoteling

Penguin is committed to publishing works of quality and integrity.
In that spirit, we are proud to offer this book to our readers:
however, the story, the experiences, and the words
are the author's alone.

To Ben

CONTENTS

Portions of the following essays
were previously published on *The Gloss.*

"The Man Who Forged a Dildo in His Own Image"

"So You've Caused an Abortion"

"Hitting on Girls in Bars"

"Breeding"

NIGHT TERRORS

NIGHTMARES

Growing up, I used to have weird sexual fantasies about my dog. In retrospect, they were probably just weird sexual fantasies about peanut butter. As much as people hate to admit or even talk about, kids start developing sexually a long way before puberty. I don't mean that they become sexually attractive or start cruising or anything, I mean that every now and again they get struck by some strange impulse. I remember watching *Batman: The Animated Series* at a very young age and experiencing an unsettling new sensation at Catwoman's revealing outfit—something exciting in a place that never had much personality before. I used to wait for the show to come on and pray to God it would be a Catwoman episode, but it never worked because I don't actually believe in God, so He probably saw right through that.

What I'm trying to say is that it's uncomfortable to talk about but kids play doctor and try to look at each other's junk all the time because kids are just tiny, crazy versions of people. They have all the same base impulses and pathological self-interest, but they're really frank about it because they haven't learned that you can't rub your crotch on stuff whenever you want to. The civilized world has suppressed most of those base impulses in adults, but they're all right there, inside every child.

When my cousin was six years old she used to disappear from family gatherings and stick a pencil in herself. Everyone else would be sitting around the table and then she'd come back brandishing it, inviting people to "smell [her] perfume" and all the family members would just look aside or stifle sobs. I don't know if her sexual development was particularly odd or if she ever graduated to Sharpies or highlighters or something a little less junior varsity, but I'm not saying it's not disturbing. I'm just saying it happens.

When I was a really little kid, I was madly in love with Luke Skywalker because he was so pure and good, like a Ken doll with a bowl cut. But right about age ten or so, I started thinking Han Solo was the more charming and interesting of the two. This is because Luke represents chastity and virtue while Han Solo represents cock. I mention this because I was still a few years off hitting puberty, but I somehow sensed that Han's dangerous virility was more appealing.

Since I was a weird, friendless kid, I thought obsessively about these kinds of things as they happened. I still followed the impulses because I wasn't quite sure what they were or where they came from, but I always felt extremely guilty about them. Once when I was about eight, I covered a whole stack of drawing paper in sketches of naked people. My mother found them and flipped out. She plucked up this one of a woman's naked torso and demanded I tell her what it was. I think she was very afraid. I said the drawing was unfinished and hurriedly drew the face of a cartoon dog over it, the breasts being its gigantic bulging eyes, the nipples its pupils. My mom seemed to buy my story because she dropped the subject but she still wore a look of incredulity, the kind of incredulity that can only come from watching your eight-year-old frantically draw a dog's face over a pair of tits. It's likely she just didn't want to believe I'd blown through three hundred sheets of paper on crudely imagined smut, but it's possible I fooled her because I'm really talented and good at drawing. To this day, I'm not entirely sure how I did it, because that cartoon dog with its giant bulging tit-eyes looked genuinely surprised at something out of view, as if witness to the loss of my innocence in real time. Or impressed that a prepubescent experiment with adult sexuality can be set aside by the collision of improvisation and denial.

None of that really gets at what I mean better than the fact that, growing up, I used to have a weird recurring sexual nightmare about Prince. The Artist. The one who wrote and recorded "Pussy Control." He also starred in *Purple Rain* and *Under the Cherry Moon*.

I don't mean that I was some kind of disaffected urban baby like those little kids whose parents are writers or architects or cartographers and they wear miniature ascots and aren't allowed to have gluten. It wasn't like that at all; it's not that Prince or some similar intangible presence would seep along my dreamscapes in which I'd be picking hot dog flowers with Turgenev and Billy Squier and then Thomas Aquinas would be like, "Where are my puddings? Who ate all my puddings?" and we'd laugh and late eighties corporate rock would filter across the hot dog meadow and it would be extremely funny because Thomas Aquinas was a fat bitch.

This wasn't the case because little kids don't understand irony; their tiny brains are stupid. Children are annoying and crazy and half-evolved sexually and practically no one in the world becomes tolerable until at least twenty-four. Everybody knows this but there will always be people who lie about it, like the ones you meet in college who swear on their packs of additive-free cigarettes they've been listening to the Modern Lovers and Can and Wire since they were eleven. Believe me, they are all self-mythologizing assholes and if you see pictures of them in middle school, you'll swiftly deduce they were exclusively concerned with WrestleMania and masturbating. Likewise, when I was a little kid, I didn't know anything about irony. My only interests were in picking my nose and getting aroused to *Batman* (probably because it was so atmospheric). My recurring sexual nightmare about Prince was genuine.

It always began with me standing in the garage, alone. I'd be looking down the steep driveway from the house where I grew up in Northern California. I spent most of my time alone as a kid, so this wasn't all that strange, but something would strike me and I'd stand and turn and gaze off a long way. Then I'd realize I could just make out faint strains of music in the distance. I would pause, disquieted there, and everything would become very still like the way it gets before earthquakes. Then I would hear cruel laughter as the music became louder and I would feel the urge to flee. The odor of evil carried even on that brisk Wine Country breeze.

The chase would begin in the way you fathom events as they unfold in dreams because pervasive dread informs you: suddenly, I would be on my tricycle, handlebar streamers flying. My pudgy, uneven little legs peddled urgently and I'd look over my shoulder to see nothing. Nothing. Still, my panic would mount. I could hear my heartbeat, hear the blood churn in my ears.

The perspective would shift and behind me he would rise: Prince, on a colossal tricycle of his own design, purple and garishly decorated, leading a parade float, his minions dancing and fornicating in the tissue blossoms. The sky would darken and he would be there—the Purple One!—rising larger and larger still, his ass cheeks naked and full each time he pedaled with heaving menace in his lace chaps. I did not understand the things he said or sang or why he gesticulated so feyly but I did understand he was coming for me.

My desperate peddling could not be enough and was never enough. The dream would end just as the giant tricycle and what it represented engulfed me. The vision would dissipate and I'd awaken, shaking, to the faint sound of his effervescent laughter. I was never sure what Nightmare Prince intended to do to me (specifically) but I knew that it would be erotic and strange and transgressive and I'm still unsure if any of this makes me racist. In this way, he was kind of a dark messenger from the realm of adulthood, intending to ferry away my innocence like some sort of silken Charon with his butt showing.

I am certain the dream postponed my adolescence a few

months longer, thanks to the correlation between sex and horror. I didn't realize that the Prince nightmare was really a nightmare about sex itself, that my kid brain had churned out an impressively lazy and no less bizarre metaphor, a flamboyant harbinger of puberty several years before it would take place. Not only does this indicate kids have sexual inclinations and awareness and curiosity before their bodies begin to reflect that, what's more is kids can be terrorized by the idea of fucking before they have any idea what it is.

I had this nightmare six or seven times from about age seven until I hit the age when you start getting really into Prince and realize *Sign 'O' the Times* is a phenomenal album. I mention all this because I recently had a dream in which I had pretty graphic sex with Prince and it actually wasn't weird. Well, I mean it was obviously weird once I woke up and thought about it, but while it was happening it seemed reasonable. I guess that's what it means to be a grown-up.

HOW I GOT KICKED
OUT OF CATECHISM

There are but a few glorious years of life when you are a sentient being but you genuinely do not know what sex is. On the cusp of that recognition, I dreamed of Prince because I instinctively knew to be afraid of sex in a deep, primitive way and Prince represented all that and more: not just what was appealing about sex but actually everything. Prince was an amalgam of man and woman and leather and lace, of breeding and orifices and incense, of sweat and perfume and paisley and butt. Once you could get to puberty, you'd refine those recognitions and be able to find them exhilarating, as is the case with learning to love Han Solo. But until then, sex is just this big purple Jungian k-hole and—also just like Prince—it's horrifying.

There is an interesting moment in between, though, the

activity of transition. If loving Luke Skywalker is perfect childhood innocence, then being afraid of Prince is what happens before you understand sex but you know it's there (last, you hit puberty, fall for Han Solo and never look back). For the moment, we're interested in that middle area, the process of learning to comprehend sex: the time when you don't know what it is, you know it's bad and you're obsessed with it.

About all you know is that it has to do with your privates. Problem is, you're a little kid. As far as you're concerned, your asshole and your genitals are exactly the same. As a teenager, I once babysat an extremely intelligent eight-year-old boy who would come out of the bathroom and announce, "I just had sex." He hadn't, of course; he'd urinated. But it was about this age that he began to know that rustling in those organs was somehow provocative, despite having no literal understanding of the sex act. Though I guess he very well could have been having sex. It's not like I was a good babysitter.

Like many girls, I quickly grasped the concept that the asshole and genitals are different opera boxes in the same theater. This didn't accelerate my understanding of sex any, though, because my rapidly evanescing search became impeded by an equally stupid association: I was right about it having to do with genitals and I knew it was very bad, so I concluded that sex was about suffering. This developmental tangent led to my getting kicked out of catechism at age eight. If you ever asked me what irony is and had a few minutes, I'd probably tell you the following story. Afterward I'd admit I don't really understand irony as a concept and am reluctant to use the word in casual conversation.

Despite our fancy heart of Wine Country location, my family was middle class. When I was a very little kid, my father delivered mail and my mom managed an orthodontist's office, answering phones and overseeing appointments. I have three half-siblings, but they were all old enough to have moved out. This left my parents in a bit of a bind for cheap daycare. Luckily, my father's parents were absolutely fucking crazy Catholic nightmare people.

My father didn't like his parents—and rightly so, because they were horrible. My grandfather was a brutish, abusive, alcoholic monster and my grandmother was a vain, ruthless, brittle harpy. I don't really want to blame them for their hateful comportment; apparently they met at some kind of USO show where my grandfather was a sailor and my grandmother was a good-time gal. She got pregnant; he left the state; she followed him halfway across the country. When she showed up at his doorstep, his racist Irish family flipped out that he'd knocked up an Italian Jew and ostracized them both until they moved back to San Francisco. I guess that means I have pluck in my genes. Pluck and resentment.

As a child, I disliked them immensely. The only thing I disliked more than them was their house: two stories of dust-suffocated Christian iconography, packed so densely into every space that if you were to be blindfolded, set at random in any room and spun three times, then removed the blindfold, there, in front of you, would be some reminder of Christ's suffering. There were remarkably gruesome crucifixes in every room, year-round nativities, baskets of half-made rosaries, a television that seemed to only flicker with muted images of Charlton Heston as Moses, stations of the cross lining every ceiling and a multitude of statues, each one more frightening than the last. The one I despised most was of Mary, right at the front door, a kind of gory warning to abandon all hope ye whose parents cannot afford decent daycare. She was about three feet in height and wearing a sky-blue cloak, palms prayered, eyes closed in an expression of blank piousness, and then—grotesquely—a bloated serpent weaving about her bare feet, forked tongue testing the curve of her toes. Last of all, the entire house smelled lushly sour from the residents' decades of mutual antipathy. It was the most frightening environment imaginable for a little kid who had excitingly theatric sexual nightmares.

My parents weren't religious at all, bless them. There was never, ever any concept of God in my house, so I passed through those crucial developmental years unencumbered by visions of a heaven full with birthday presents and candy. This is why I'm neither religious nor an atheist.

I mention all of this because as much as my father had a strained relationship with his own parents, they did offer an alluringly free alternative to daycare: catechism class. Yes, my grandparents were dead set on indoctrinating the Cardiff children and their equally strapped-for-cash neighbors by providing daycare at the low, low price of feeling vaguely guilty about orgasms for the rest of their lives. They brought some church lady to do the teaching, while my grandfather worked and my grandmother kept an all-seeing eye on us from the kitchen. So, although I barely knew my grandparents and didn't know what Jesus was, around age eight my parents started dropping me off at a fetid murder house for seven straight hours of Bible learning.

At first, it wasn't so bad, because the Bible is frequently great. If you cut out all the lineage tables and nonsense and barbarism and passages that contradict each other, you're left with dozens of beautiful, incomparably elegant stories, one of my favorite books, and about a hundred pages. Even better, the stories are insane, so they're fascinating to little kids (who are also insane). I just latched on to all the wrong things. This, you'll find, is a recurring theme.

The stories about original sin, for example, were my favorite because the Garden of Eden sounded like a place where you not only lived in harmony with every cool animal ever, but you could also watch trees replenish fruit as you ate it and, I suspected, probably even breathe under water. Adam and Eve's nakedness was presented as innocent and natural and beautiful, which—in my eight-year-old brain—made sense only if they were giant babies. When I'd prompt the teacher again and again to tell the story of Adam and Eve, she was delighted I'd taken such a shine to one of the more important stories of the Old Testament. What she didn't realize was I thought it was about huge infants communicating with animals telepathically. This speaks to a lifelong problem of selective interpretation and stupidity, which has variously led me to believe that *Lord of the Flies* is about how fun it would be to not have parents and that *Death in Venice* proves everyone looks hot in a Breton shirt.

It couldn't last for long, of course, because at a certain point they were going to start expecting me to believe, though I had no intention of ingesting it seriously. That, in conjunction with my attention span glutted on television and video games, would lead my mind to wander. When storytime was over and we were expected to talk about the moral quality of what we'd heard, I kind of just checked out. The teacher soon noticed my glazed affect—a terrible confluence of unwillingness to participate and the permanent expression of witless fatuity I have on my face to this day—and began prompting me with statements like, "Ashley, did you have something you wanted to say?"

The first few weeks, I got by on my enthusiasm for wanting to hear new stories and it was all people living inside whales and having leprosy. That enthusiasm began to dissolve as we veered into the endless lists of rules about what you could and couldn't do and getting stoned to death for having sex while menstruating. Then I just sat in catechism class wondering what the Ninja Turtles were up to. Both the teacher and my grandmother noticed my engagement waning and, one month in, I was ID'd as a problem child. Fair enough.

One day, while bored at the table, I absentmindedly exclaimed, "Oh my God, I'm missing [some cartoon]." I was given an hour-long time-out in a darkened room, seated at the intersection of two plain white walls, for taking the Lord's name in vain. It was then I realized these fuckers were pretty hard-bitten and, if I ever wanted to get out of there and be home where I could watch TV for as long as I wanted and say swears, I was going to have to fight back.

Luckily, if you want to freak Catholics out, the best way to do that is be a child discovering what sex is.

We're still very early on in this book, so now's probably a good time to break the fourth or third wall/go behind the curtain or green door and say all the stories in this book are true. Plenty of details, however, have been obscured. That's for a single reason: to protect the friends, family and enemies who wish to remain anonymous and won't be sold out, because I would lose my mind if they did it to me. If you're the sort of person who gets outraged by things like this, then your extremely literal brain is going to keep you from enjoying this very book in addition to many other things in life, like blog posts with which you disagree. Still, it's time to reiterate that nothing in here is made up. Not because I think lying is immoral—lying is *fucking fun*—but because I'm contractually obligated to write nonfiction.

This is all a roundabout way of saying we've come to the first part of this book in which I've wanted to lie a little and say that as a young kid, I crafted a sophisticated multiphasic plan of attack against my horrible Catholic grandmother, but after much time at the gym and soul searching and whiskey, I couldn't really come up with a compelling, funny series of offensives so I'll just be straight with you: I drew dirty pictures.

There was a time after each catechism class, the last part of the day and eventually the only hour I looked forward to, in which we were allowed to draw ("free draw") the feelings and emotions inspired by that day's lesson. If that sounds pretty progressive, it's not because my grandmother and the teacher wanted us children to express ourselves artistically—no, with the exception of the Renaissance and shit like that, art is pretty much always the enemy of religion—but because you can only fill so many hours of the day with Bible stories.

In fact, they couldn't even do that, so most days began

with several hours of stories from the Bible and accompanying discussion, then transitioned into this terrible pop Christianity appropriate for eight-year-olds. They were "nowadays stories," which were basic Bible parables with an infusion of cool modern stuff like BMX bikes and sexy young rebels in polo shirts explaining to their stuffy old science teachers that evolution is a sham. Somehow, these two parts of the day (with a brief break for lunch) managed to take something like seven hours. If anything, the free drawing portion of the day was meant for working out frustrations. I had a lot of those.

We kids—mostly my cousins and a few poor neighbors—were pretty much left to our own devices during this hour, in which we sat at the kitchen table and illustrated our feelings about catechism while my grandmother and the teacher took a much-needed break to be embittered and hateful. After a few weeks I realized I could draw anything I wanted; the teacher never even looked at it before I stuffed it into the kitchen cabinet reserved expressly for this purpose. Which meant I could amass a portfolio. Of art.

It started off pretty innocent and pretty literal, with Leviathan risen from rolling ocean waves, heaving its gargantuan body onto the sand and, one by one, mauling each rabbi that had the hubris to tell Job why God had forsaken him. I drew another of Leviathan belching rabbi parts amid buzzing flies. I really liked Job, so I drew some portraits of him in a loincloth with a sword and flowing hair that crowned his face full of leprosy and he stood over a pile of sexy harem girls with their tits out (the sexy harem girls also had leprosy, so he wouldn't feel bad). I drew the giant babies Adam and Eve stomping out of the Garden of Eden and leaving a trail of broken animal bodies in their wake in an act of defiance I felt they deserved; God's the one who put the tree in there in the first place.

Soon I suspected that, if caught, the violence and suggestiveness weren't going to get me kicked out of catechism the way I wanted, but would probably just earn me more time in the dark room, staring at the corner, which, for the developing neurotic, is a horrible punishment. Pretty swiftly I graduated to drawing pictures of Satan and the angel Gabriel swordfighting with their huge penises (or "peepees," to employ the parlance of the age) but I'd only really seen little kid penises, so they looked like coconuts with fingers sticking out of them. In another, a victorious Satan looming over Gabriel and urinating on his broken body with great sexual menace. I drew the angels in Sodom having sex with Lot's daughters, or what I imagined that would be, which really just amounted to drawing them pressed against each other because, at eight, I obviously had no concept of penetration. Perhaps my favorite was a drawing of Cain, naked and mowing down a field of wheat, slicing his brother Abel in half with lasers that issued from his nipples, because I thought lasers coming out of his mouth would be too weird.

The day it all went down, though, I remember one drawing the best. Strangely, it was inspired by that afternoon's modern-day story, which concerned a young fighter pilot who was handsome and gifted. One day, while flying, he accidentally did a flip in the air. He was so exhilarated by the trick that he did another. The high of doing these flips in his plane overtook him and he began to do more and more, until he lost control. And crashed. And died. It was about hubris, obviously, a popular subject for modern Christian allegories because all the stories in the Bible about being venal, ostentatious or consumptive are harder to sell nowadays. In retrospect, I often wonder why they didn't just tell the story of Icarus, which is more effective and elegant. I suppose they didn't because a regular guy flying a regular airplane is more interesting to children than ancient peoples crafting magnificent feathered wing contraptions and flying into the goddamn sun. Or because it's pagan, which is actually the reason.

Anyway, that day's drawing concerned our friend the pilot after he'd crash-landed. In my artistic expression, the plane lay broken and smoldering in a fetid swamp, our tragic protagonist consumed alive by piranha. I figured, if they were going to punish the poor guy just for having fun in his airplane, why not go the extra mile and really show his suffering? The offending portion of the image showed the pilot, lifeless in the waters, missing approximately half of himself as two piranha fought over his genitals. I remember, as I was drawing the teeth gnashing through flesh, thinking I may have actually gone too far. *I'm in the Lord's summer house*, I thought, *and I might actually get in trouble, in a spiritual way, for what I'm doing.* In the subsequent moments of terror, I realized that catechism was working. Then I realized that if God existed he'd be the reason I was able to draw such great pictures, so I smiled to myself and shaded some bloody testicle parts floating in the bog.

My work was done when I figured it wasn't going to get much darker than fish eating a man's genitals. I stood up, retrieved the rest of my portfolio from the cabinet, slid my newest creation in and waited. When my grandmother and the teacher returned to the kitchen, I stood up again, walked between them and, in what must have been preposterously exaggerated slapstick, dropped the portfolio on the kitchen floor. Months of explicit, disturbing, disgusting visions spilled all over. My grandmother and the teacher knelt down to help me pick them up.

I did, in fact, get the corner that day and sat there alone under one dust-caked station of the cross, waiting for my parents to come get me. I distracted myself by thinking about catching up on all the cartoons I'd missed over the past few months. I heard my dad pull up outside and ring the doorbell, but then it was a long time before anyone came and got me.

The car ride home was mostly silent and, to this day, I'm not sure what my grandmother told my father. The only thing said I can remember was at one point I declared into silence, "Dad, I don't want to see Grandma anymore."

My dad said, "Why's that, Ash?"

I said, "I don't like her."

My father nodded and I didn't see her again until she was on her deathbed (where she still sucked).

It may sound kind of disturbing that my recalcitrance took the form of graphically depicted sexual violence, but it's not as though I was off in a field torturing cats and making necklaces out of their bones. I was behaving in a way to get a specific response and using images I faintly understood to be provocative, though not why. By eight years old, children know that sex is a thing and that it exists; they just don't know the particulars. Laser nipples and piranhas eating genitals are actually quite consistent with how many children engage with the concept of sexuality. I even have to be somewhat impressed with myself that, at age eight, I managed to use sex as a psychological weapon, which puts me pretty far ahead of the curve as girls go.

THE FIRST TIME I SAW PORN

People often say that the modern world or this culture and that industry are "saturated with sex." I'm inclined to believe this isn't true because it wasn't long ago that women were regularly married off at twelve. That's a culture saturated with sex, when it's acceptable to fuck children.

Despite what they said about suggestively wholesome teen pop singers and hot shorts marketed to little girls, my generation wasn't saturated with sex. We were tormented by it. Sex haunted our steps like a distant noise of flesh slapping against flesh or an ouroboros that penetrates itself over your shoulder while you are little and trying to fingerpaint. That is, until I crossed the threshold and sex was no longer an ineffable thing. The fastest, most brutal and heartless way of passing from the stage of not knowing to the next is to witness sex, which is to say, discover pornography. A ruinous passing it was.

It happened on my ninth birthday. I was a friendless kid, as I've mentioned, thanks in part to my debilitating social anxiety, weird affectations and general physical discomfort. Those, in turn, were exacerbated by being about a foot taller than every other kid my age and also by my mother relentlessly pressuring me about the importance of popularity. Luckily, at nine years old, many of a child's social habits are still determined by parents so, even though I didn't have any friends, my birthday would roll around and six or seven little girls my age would materialize.

Unfortunately, the established social hierarchies of the blacktop didn't just go away because you were shuttled over to someone's house. Basically, my ninth birthday slumber party involved all the things I hated about the school day: girls my age ignoring me, ridiculing me, avoiding me, talking about me like I wasn't there, and doing cool shit they sloughed off as soon as I expressed approval or interest.

Leading the pack was Sarah Gill, not necessarily one of the popular girls at school (there isn't really a quantifiable measure of popularity until breasts develop) but one of the cool ones. She was really pretty and blond and wore low-slung pants and the boys would let her and her alone play kickball or basketball with them. As soon as Sarah Gill got dropped off at my house, she looked around the room, sized up the competition, and immediately established herself as the leader. Pretty soon, they were all playing MASH with each other and talking about school politics and I just sat off a ways, feeling a mixture of grief at being alienated in my own home and gratefulness at being included even tangentially.

By the time we were all huddled in sleeping bags in the

living room, waiting for my parents to go to bed, Sarah's aggressive assertion of authority over me had become almost theatrical. It turned out she had brought a Discman and some CDs (I guess because she figured she'd need a backup if things got really boring) (I'm still astonished by how cool this nine-year-old was) so there she sat in her sleeping bag talking about this band the Beatles and this album *Sgt. Pepper's*. Her favorite song was called "Lucy in the Sky with Diamonds," and she was giddily sharing the headphones, ear beside ear, with every other girl in attendance but myself. I'd say I wanted to listen and she'd say, "You probably wouldn't like it," and then whoever was her current partner would express outlandish approval—"That's probably the best song ever made"— and Sarah would nod and offer some profound insight: "You know it's about drinking alcohol, right?"

Even at the time I couldn't really begrudge Sarah for snubbing me this way because kids, whether nine or fifteen, can craft social humiliation out of toothpaste if it's all they have. I was effectively used to this kind of thing. Lucky for me, it was easy to seize social cachet as a nine-year-old: just as my parents went to bed, they handed me a bowl of popcorn and the remote. Sarah's Discman saw a rapid devaluation of the social currency it had only moments ago. I'd become the sheriff of this town.

Predictably, it was great. It was also the last time I was ever the coolest person in the room.

We started off the night with a pay-per-view movie that I don't remember. At this point I should say we had a black box acquired through some distant family member, so when I say "pay-per-view" I mean not paying per view. I mean stealing views. The black box unscrambled every channel, even the super premium ones that would show movies all day long and then after about one a.m. become adult channels. I had never stayed up late enough and unsupervised enough to really know what an "adult" channel was; I had just once or twice experienced the moment they switched over, when one movie ended and suddenly the sets and lighting of the next seemed suspiciously lower in production value. It was at this point some nearby adult, a parent or older sibling, would audibly gasp "Oh!" and change the channel, confirming the switch-over represented something abundantly interesting.

There I was, popcorn bowl and remote in hand, dictating what we watched, and all the girls were vying to sit next to me. I knew it was an empty victory but it was still pretty thrilling to feel like people wanted my attention. Naturally, Sarah Gill shoved her way right to the center of the circle and parked herself beside me, because if she couldn't be the alpha female, she was going to be second in command.

"We should watch [whatever movie from the stack my parents had rented for us]. That'd be really cool. Have you seen that movie, Ashley? It's really cool."

"Yeah, I totally have," I said and I assume I was lying, "It's pretty cool, but I'd totally watch it again in case the rest of you haven't seen it."

"Cool," said Sarah.

I left the channel on pay-per-view and summoned one of the other girls to go get said movie from the stack on the counter. Let's say it was *Free Willy*, which would be eerily appropriate, if it weren't so asinine. We watched the movie and it must have been about one thirty when the credits rolled. Banter was exchanged about how cool this or that was, how "fine" such and such lead was, what we enjoyed from the soundtrack, and so on. At this point, I was probably feeling as good as a nine-year-old could feel without getting a pony. Not only was I staying awake really late, but I had this whole group of peers actually lobbying for my attention because I, for the first time ever, was in control of what we as a social system were doing.

Then it all went to shit.

I hit Stop on the remote and wriggled out of my sleeping bag to fetch the video. We were immediately transported back to the television, to the black box still at channel 99. The set was a quaint Christmas scene, with a sleigh in the background, a full red sack bulging with (presumably) toys, a pine tree decorated seasonally, and a completely disgusting, tattoo-clotted dirtbag pounding out an equally repulsive giant-titted siren, bent over the front of the ornate red sleigh. Neither member of the couple involved was dressed as a Christmas character. I am unsure if she was supposed to be Mrs. Claus or a "naughty" girl, just as I'm unsure if he was supposed to be Santa or an elf or a reindeer. Both of them were naked but for her Lucite heels. The only thing Christmas-themed about the central characters was located between her tan, sinewy thighs: she had a clitoris piercing, from which swung a classic cherry-red Christmas tree ornament, the kind you see families lovingly hooking to branches in holiday coffee commercials, and it swung from his balls to her belly like some shining pendulum of forsaken childhood. Also, it was March.

Before I could leap back to the remote and change the channel, I was swept away in what I saw and this, I can reasonably say, was probably the moment that marked my first real psychological snap. I stood tall among a group of elementary school girls huddled in sleeping bags watching this disgusting display and I thought to myself . . . *That's it?!*

And then: *That's what I get for surviving adolescence? That's what this life of alienation and humiliation and self-loathing and public torment is hurtling toward? That's what it means to be an adult? Someday I, too, will be bent over and squealing like a sow on a slaughterhouse floor while some grim-faced refrigerator of bulbous muscles and leathery skin that weeps off in folds smashes his vein-suffocated manhood into me from behind, grunting and pulling at my swollen breasts?* . . . Only dumb, how a nine-year-old would think it.

It was at this point that she scooted into the sleigh and turned on her back, putting her feet into the air. His hulking carriage barely accounted for the change in placement as he continued to joylessly hack away. I will always remember her shoes, commonly referred to as "stripper shoes," a towering clear platform with a burst of white fluffy material across the toe. I fixated on them, drowning in horror, that someday I would have to endure this and furthermore would have to lie back, watching my feet shake up and down in high heels with little fuzzy pom-poms on them.

It was a dense darkness that came over me. I'd never experienced greater antipathy in my life. Here again, I thought to myself, *No.*

The camera suddenly fixated on her little clitoris ornament and zoomed in with its unwavering lecherous gaze until all we could see was the glistening shaft of his penis and the incoherent bouncing of the little red ball. She shrieked and shrieked.

One cry was so blood-curdling that the spell broke and I realized I was still surrounded by my classmates. I grabbed the remote just as Sarah Gill grabbed my pant leg, her eyes rapt on the television, and she said with the same blank, affected worldliness with which she said everything, "That's a cute ornament."

As if the idea dawning—this is what sex looks like—hadn't been practically voluptuous in its horror, I then had to realize I was completely fucking alone in recognizing what we'd just seen. I knew it was sex and not a single one of the other girls had come to that same conclusion. Yes, as soon as the popcorn was gone and I was relinquished of the remote, not only would this false camaraderie evaporate, but I would also be separate from them developmentally. I could never go back to the world of believing in man's goodness.

We watched another movie, mostly in silence. Then we all fell asleep. The next day, we went back to our respective homes, and the day after that, we went back to our respective social stations.

I didn't really care as much as I had before, though, because it was in that moment of watching the little ornament waggle back and forth—in the very moment I distinctly remember thinking that her labia looked like turkey spilling out of a sandwich—that I somehow became a little older than the rest. If Sarah Gill, the most cosmopolitan of the group, could look on that image and see nothing but a prop in a vacuum, then every last one of them were still affixed to a place that I, for some reason, had been severed from. Because of this, the teasing didn't smart quite the same way it had before. Plus, I learned a valuable lesson: don't let children watch hard-core pornography. Which is a lesson a lot of people don't have to learn, but life is about the journey.

MY FAMILY'S HOMEMADE SEX TAPES

I've been an insomniac my whole life. I don't have the kind of insomnia that affects sleep itself; when I do sleep, I sleep fine. I have the kind where you can't get there. Which is to say, I don't really have insomnia so much as I have anxiety.

I just lie in bed for hours, worrying ceaselessly about everything in the world. When I was really little, I'd worry about something living in the closet and I'd fill in the horror blanks with little bits I'd picked up from edited-for-television versions of movies like *It* and *The Shining*. As an adolescent, I worried about social politics. In college, I fretted about home invasion and dying in a plane crash and violent murder. Since graduating, I've had terrible recurring nightmares wherein the administration discovers I haven't gone to math class for an entire year and forces me to repeat the whole thing lest they revoke my degree, which makes me nostalgic for the plane crash visions. In ten years, it will be stomach cancer and under-eye bags.

I can worry with the best of them: I've never been the first in a pool for fear of invisible, chlorine-adapted great white sharks. Whenever I say anything bad about someone, I experience a flash of crippling paranoia that somehow my phone has accidentally dialed that person in my pocket and he or she has heard everything. I don't go on roller coasters and I wonder if all my friends secretly hate me. I refuse to take out my trash at night because I'm afraid of mountain lions (I live in Brooklyn). I'm so afraid of home invasion I'd put padlocks on my cereal boxes if I could. I'm horrified by children in formal wear. I worry when I'm at the gym that someone on the treadmill next to me can smell my vagina. I worry they think it smells like a pet store. Or a marina. Or cleaning a deep fryer. When a trailer for a horror movie comes on at a theater, I cover my eyes *and* plug my ears. Just the other night I was lying awake in a sweat thinking about this movie where maneless lions stalk Val Kilmer in a region of Kenya called Tsavo. I'm petrified of the idea of getting mauled to death by maneless lions but I was just as disturbed that his manager would let him make a decision like that and also by the concept of fame (which sounds like a prison!).

But almost nothing in the world keeps me awake at night more than the idea of my high school boyfriend filming us having sex unbeknownst to me. Nothing. This is the most suffocating dread in my life. I have considered emailing him, even though we haven't spoken in years, just to confirm that he didn't. The problem is, there's no real way to word that.

Granted, the idea of being even a willing participant in a sex tape terrifies me. All I'd need is a single glimpse of stretch mark or stomach roll or an unflattering angle and my clitoris would retract into my abdomen forever and just live in there, devoting itself to God or philosophy or becoming a chess grand master and never coming back out under any circumstances. I also have no idea what my vulva looks like and I'd prefer to keep it that way because you can never love someone if you know for certain your genitals look like a Scotch egg halved lengthwise. Which is a frightening possibility, if porn is to be believed.

I can't even have sex with the lights on. Boyfriends will press for this and I always straighten my shoulders in a very serious way and explain slowly that having sex with the lights on is like kissing with your eyes open and the very suggestion of sex you can see is unromantic, awkward, even strange. I manage to make this sound extremely reasonable. This is a good angle: when someone says something that frightens you, just make them feel judged. Usually they stop because they're weak. Well, weaker.

It's not that my fear of being filmed surreptitiously is informed purely by hatred for my weird, doughy, unphotogenic body. The real problem—and I'm being honest—is sex that is genuinely good seldom looks good. Performance sex is acrobatic and straining and meant to be regarded (that is to say porn) and porn stars don't look like they're having any fun! Which is super glib of me. Good sex involves all kinds of ugly positioning and bent abdomens. I haven't even touched on the

subject of the faces people make when they're actually enjoying sex. It's not a very complicated subject that needs much
explication, though: they look fucking ridiculous.

I have no reason to think my first boyfriend filmed us,
other than the fact he was a teenager with a bunch of technol-
ogy at his fingertips. It's possible that my anxiety has increased
over the years simply because we have grown apart, but I frequently lie awake at night worrying there's a grainy video out
there, taken from a cracked closet door under a sweater. The
possibility of this is far worse than being eaten by maneless
lions and approximately one-third as erotic.

My horror at sex tapes started well before I ever had sex.
It was Thanksgiving Day, my favorite day of the year,
when one's appetite and one's guilt of gluttony are at their
most extreme inverse. Thanksgiving was my favorite day because my parents and I would go to my aunt's house, where
much of the family would converge; a magical place where you
could eat foods by the handful (even pie) from noon until
night. My family was also of the opinion that kids should be
able to hold their liquor and there's really only one way to
learn.

On this Thanksgiving, when I was about twelve, I was
entrusted with filming the day's activities. I was using a camera belonging to the eldest of my three cousins, who was
about thirty. We'll call him Frank. Frank was perhaps my
favorite cousin because he was a bit of a delinquent and drove
a cool motorcycle and listened to the Beastie Boys and read
skateboarding magazines. He'd drink only forties of Mickey's
and one time, when my family was staying at his cabin in the

woods, he woke up my parents and me by announcing he hoped none of us had gotten pregnant the night before; he'd "been doing some drinking." I was about seven when that happened, so I found him extremely cool.

Despite the honor of videographer duties, I was getting pretty loaded on Jack and Coke because, really, if there's a better drink for children, I haven't thrown it up. I was wandering around the house, cocktail in one hand, camera in the other, swaying drunk because the adults monitored the children's drinking by doing the mixing themselves, a system I ably circumvented by being tall enough to reach the alcohol. That concoction sloshed ruefully with a half pound of boiled shrimp cocktail inside me, further exacerbated by motion sickness from *Sonic the Hedgehog 2*.

I'd spent much of the day approaching family members and asking them to offer their Thanksgiving well wishes while experimenting with cool sideways camera angles. Within about an hour, I'd started to think of myself as a regular Godard because everything I did was affected and indulgent. Convinced that I was a budding auteur, I captured the turkey's odyssey from counter to oven in oscillating close-ups from bizarre angles. I filmed my littlest cousins playing video games and swinging in the hammock outside. I filmed my dad stirring flour into gravy and my aunts being bitches over mimosas.

Just before dinner, I could sense I'd overdone it. Because I'd been entrusted with the camera, an extremely adult responsibility, I wasn't about to demonstrate my youth with a parabola of vomit over the tablecloth. In my drunken state, I concluded that slugging a gallon of water beside the toilet would somehow draw attention. I slipped out into the garage, where there stood a refrigerator for soda, beer and bottled water, and sat down on the cold cement beside Frank's beloved motorcycle to spend a few minutes collecting myself.

It appeared to have been a false alarm. I took a few bottles of water from the fridge and chugged them, then felt pretty fine and decided to review my work. I flipped the camera on and rewound a bit. I checked the tape, saw I was nearing the beginning but not quite there, and went back to rewinding. A minute later, I pressed Play.

There came a sight that may haunt me to my grave: my cousin Frank's wife, head between (presumably) his legs, gulping down his engorged pink cock. She made eye contact with the camera for a single piercing moment and then breached over his shaft. I turned it off immediately, turned my head to the side and vomited down the entire length of Frank's obsessively shined red motorcycle.

I was upset by what I'd seen but I knew I'd have to clean up the mess before I did anything about it. I returned to the refrigerator and discovered that I had consumed the last of the water, so I did what any drunk witless twelve-year-old who'd just watched her cousin's wife give him a blowjob on camera would: I washed my vomit off his motorcycle with Mountain Dew. The chemical smell of neon soda wasn't doing my upset stomach any favors, but I slicked off most of the puke and dispersed it with my shoes and still more cans of Dew.

After I'd kicked the vomit around the garage, I opened the side door to let some air in. I then realized I'd gotten a small aquarium's worth of shrimp-Coke puke on my shirt, which I was also forced to rinse away with soda. This is invariably what I think of when I hear the brand's slogan "Do the Dew."

I sat down again to think things through. If I had one certainty, it was that I couldn't just return to my family's Thanksgiving celebration like everything was normal. If anything, I couldn't look Frank's wife in the face across a beautiful turkey spread knowing full well his penis had been in her mouth like that.

An intense impulse to judge them both swept over me and I concluded they must be taken to task for their appalling behavior. I was furious at the injustice of having to see such an intimate moment and the only thing that outweighed my fury was fear I'd done something terrible and was going to get in trouble. I was also still very drunk and smelled like a Red Lobster bathroom. But I was going to confront Frank because it just didn't seem right to bottle my outrage.

Thankfully, I didn't decide that the best way to do that was over dinner surrounded by family. I marched inside and grabbed my second-eldest cousin—Frank's sister, Stacy— and told her we needed to have a conversation. She was on mashed potato duty, so she gave me hell about dragging her out of the kitchen but eventually followed me on account of my bizarrely secretive behavior.

I led her outside and down the driveway. When we stopped, I folded my arms in an extremely serious manner. I began by telling her I'd spent a great deal of my Thanksgiving filming the family and doing my part to commemorate the holiday. To hear my twelve-year-old self tell it, I'd sacrificed my day off to record their memories for them, like some selfless Irish monk cataloging the minutiae of civilization itself.

Before I could get any further, the third-eldest cousin, Tess, came out. She approached with a look of confusion. I paused momentarily to consider the audience, then decided the more present to hear my story, the better. I backed up and explained to Tess what a giving little videographer I'd been that day. Even now, I'm not sure if this contextualizing was pure self-righteousness or my attempt to emotionally manipulate the audience in the event I was actually in trouble for doing something bad. Also, I was pretty hammered.

Then, I told them, I'd taken a moment to reflect and rewound the camera and came upon a video. A video of Frank and his wife together. Stacy and Tess didn't understand.

"I found a tape," I repeated, thinking it explanation enough.

Nothing.

"I found a tape," with more emphasis on each word.

"What are you talking about?" Stacy asked.

It was at this point I began to shake with worry. As I have a permanently guilty conscience, it occurred to me that perhaps what I'd done was so vile and invasive they couldn't comprehend it. This was actually all my fault and was going to be a black mark on the family. I'd be exiled or given some terrible punishment and all because of an accident. This is exactly the kind of thinking that leads to fully grown adults who stay awake at night worrying about minor Val Kilmer works.

Recognition came over Stacy's face and she exclaimed, "Oh! A sex tape?! You found a sex tape?"

Just like that, my moral crusade was renewed.

"Yeah. I did," I said resolutely, nostrils flaring.

They looked at each other.

"And it's wrong," I started, "It's totally inappropriate—"

Tess burst into laughter and Stacy right along with her.

Stacy explained, "Oh come on, Ashley. My husband and I have a bunch."

"What?" *But it seemed so immoral! And gross!* "What are you talking about?"

Tess nodded. "Yeah, pretty much everyone who's married does that."

"When two people get married," Stacy continued, "they have to do all kinds of gross stuff so they don't get bored of each other."

Tess added with a grim, knowing flatness, "Sex tapes are nothing. Just wait till you grow up. You'll stop being so judgmental."

"And you'll also be really sick of having sex with your husband," said Stacy. She leaned over and examined my shoulder. "What's that green stuff all over your shirt? Oh my god. Did you throw up on yourself?"

"No!" I said and became really, really upset this time because my two adult cousins seemed suddenly more interested in the soda-flavored vomit flecked all over me than in the staggering moral failing of their brother Frank, who had not only filmed himself and his wife having sex, he'd been so devil-may-care as to forget which tape it was and let me record my littlest cousins reading picture books over their ravenous breathless fellatio.

"It isn't right!" I cried but my moral high ground was starting to give. "He shouldn't have left that tape in there."

"Jesus, Ashley," Tess said, "it's not like you can label them in an obvious way."

"Yeah, he probably just mixed them up." Stacy prodded one of the bigger stains on my shirt and added, "You should go take a bath or something. You reek."

With that, my eldest female cousins went back into the house, back to their mashed potato making and mimosa drinking, giggling to themselves about the absurdity of it all. There I was, standing in the driveway in the shadow of Stacy's SUV, my shirt smelling like the gutter of a soda fountain where a deep-sea fisherman had drowned.

In retrospect, it was a pretty formative experience. After the anger subsided and the hangover set in, I realized there's not a whole lot of truly immoral shit that can occur between two consenting adults. I also learned that there's no excuse not to creatively label your sex tapes. Maybe sad faces with tear drops? Or skulls and bones? I will remember these lessons whenever I recall the sight of Frank's wife, forever straining to hold herself there and wheezing dick with her eyes half open.

I guess my extreme reluctance to participate in a filmed sex act is informed purely by this scarring experience and maybe a little vanity, so when I tried to say all that other stuff about neurosis, it wasn't really true. Sorry for being a liar.

FIRST LOVE

I didn't really have a first love, but from a very young age it's beaten into you that first love is some touchstone you'll remember forever and never fully recover from and always look back on fondly. Only people who enjoyed having sex as teenagers can possibly feel this way. I don't mean that in a judgmental way; if people didn't want to fuck teenagers, there wouldn't be laws against it.

Most teenage sex is by design fumbling, awkward, messy, misguided, and extremely unlikely to result in female orgasm. A lot of straight girls spend a few years having sex with teenage boys, convincing themselves they're enjoying it and sifting through a mental Rolodex of sex advice from horrible magazines in an attempt to feel involved. If they're lucky, they'll go to college and meet some guy who's into having a "sexual dialogue" and reading ancient Chinese books about technique and, although that sounds insufferable, he's actually instrumental developmentally. If they're really, really lucky, they'll move on and find someone they just like having sex with. Guys, on the other hand, keep sticking themselves inside of things and they either get better or they don't. What I'm saying is that very few people actually have good sex as teenagers, but that doesn't stop nostalgia from working its insidious revisionism and sweetening it all.

Most people do, however, have that one moment where they first look on a peer and find that peer extremely interesting. More interesting than others. It usually comes out of nowhere and time stops and everything is lush and slow and there's string accompaniment.

I was in fourth grade. Because the California public school system is kind of a free-for-all and everyone's just figuring it out as they go along, we had one weekly meeting of music class. It began with all this noble ambition: trying to teach everyone an instrument, to read sheet music, to listen intelligently to *St. Matthew's Passion*. Within a few weeks they just gave up and the extent of "music class" was sitting in a circle and singing along to currently charting singles with a still-warm printout of the lyrics, which is probably a metaphor for public education if you'd like to pause and reflect for a moment.

I had a crush on a fifth grader named Derrick. He was impossibly beautiful in the way that only people younger than a fifth-grade boy are allowed to find impossibly beautiful: a basketball player, tan and athletic with a huge smile and bottomless dimples. I haven't seen him since middle school, so he kind of lives forever in my memory as being like this.

One day in class—I was in a multi-age program thanks

to progressivism—our teacher had brought in "I Swear" by All-4-One. I'm trying not to embed too much transient pop culture ephemera into any story I tell because I genuinely desire immortality, but if you've never heard this song I suggest you go and find it. You're in for a treat.

There we were, sitting in a circle under the whiteboard, printout in our hands. How this was supposed to educate or enrich us in any capacity, I cannot say. During the song's crescendo, our eyes met. Rather than look away, he seemed to look more intensely at me and I swear (*HA!*) he was singing to me and we were the only people in the room and all I could hear was the honey sweet harmony of this second-string Boyz II Men and then the sax came in and I thought he loved me back.

Later that day, I went to sit alone by a ditch. I spent most of my recesses there in elementary school. I was on the second-to-last rung of the social ladder; the only person below me was a Lithuanian exchange student with a distracting face mole. Because children are horrible, I took every opportunity to assert my station over her. I say this for two reasons: (1) I was stupid because I probably could have made friends with her and elementary school might have been a little less crushing for me and (2) it has a happy ending because when puberty hit she grew into the mole and got absurdly hot.

I liked the ditch because sometimes it was a creek and you could race paper boats by yourself, but I favored it mostly because it was a low-traffic area, which meant less scrutiny. That day, some kids were nearby having a conversation about Derrick. I crept behind the handball court to get a little closer and learned Derrick had struck up a relationship with fellow fifth grader Tabitha, a willowy, thick-haired beauty who sang and did theater and wasn't afraid of being looked at and had developed really, really early.

I was destroyed. It all made sense. Obviously Derrick had no feelings for me. The moment had been a fluke, skewed by the song's outlandish sentimentality. I crept back to social obscurity and didn't talk to anyone or have any friends and got bullied like everyone else. I carried this little wound in my chest for two more years.

In sixth grade, our school took a weekend-long field trip to a campground a few hours north. We stayed in bunk beds in gender-specific dorms and hiked and played capture the flag, and I wore a T-shirt over my bathing suit. The final night was the "big dance" and I won't patronize you by building it up any more than that.

Middle school—grades six through eight—was, in certain ways, actually more forgiving than elementary school. The kids were arguably meaner, but that wasn't going to change. The good thing, though, was the boys were starting to become interested in sex and nothing equalizes the middle school playing field like hormones. Social hierarchy was no longer exclusively determined by having the right clothes and liking the right pop culture placemakers; it was also about whether or not boys thought you were pretty. I did a little better here, owing to a growth spurt and a summer replacing meals with orange juice.

The night of the final dance, I hung along the side of the dance floor, eating snack mix and watching the kids who weren't as terrified of their peers. There are plenty of wallflowers and social outcasts at this age so I don't write this under the impression I was special, just alienated. Then I noticed Derrick was on the sidelines, too.

For some strange reason, I was compelled to approach him. It was probably fascination with the enormous disruption of social order that distracted my characteristic anxiety. I kind of danced up to him to make it look casual and tried to feel out whether or not I'd be welcome. Derrick, to his credit, was always a pretty nice kid and smiled.

"What's up?" I said, because that was how you greeted people.

"Not much. What's up with you?"

"I don't really like dancing," I said. I had also never been asked.

"Yeah, it's kind of stupid," he said.

"It's totally stupid!" I said. We agreed!

There was a long, uncomfortable beat of silence, and I remembered that I didn't know how to talk to people. He was probably wondering if I would go away or not.

"So, you sad to go home?" I asked.

"Yeah. My parents are pretty lame."

"Mine, too!"

"School's been pretty lame, too. Tabitha and I broke up last week."

"Oh. That's terrible." Exclamation points fired off inside me.

"We've been together since, like, fifth grade. It's been kind of on and off. She just wants more time to do plays, you know? She doesn't have time for a real relationship."

"Yeah, I know what it's like."

"Having a girlfriend is like having a job or something."

"Totally."

Whichever hopelessly uncool teacher was saddled with the task of deejaying this event came over the speakers to say the next song would be the last. In a remarkable but true twist of fate, it was "I Swear" by All-4-One.

My heart skipped. There's no way he remembered, of course, Derrick had probably flashed that smile at a million girls to a million different pop songs in his day. But it inspired me. "Hey . . ." I started.

"Do you have someone for the last dance?" he asked.

I tried not to show that every fiber of my being sang with joy. "No."

"Come on, let's go."

He led me out onto the dance floor and I thrilled at holding his hand. We took a place under the gentle spin of the disco ball and for a moment I felt that everyone was watching. At first I was mechanical and uncomfortable but then I fell into my own skin and his hands slipped around my lower back and I knew the next step would be putting my head on his shoulder. Just as I leaned in, I remembered what it was like to look him in the eyes from across our singing circle two years ago and I felt this was the culmination of something that had been gone in me since. Everything was going to be set right and then . . .

Someone tapped my shoulder. Not a gentle tap, but an insistent, aggressive, fingernail-forward kind of tap. I raised my head from Derrick's shoulder.

It was Tabitha. She wore an expression that seemed equal parts bridled fury and smug stillness. She looked at me and said, "Can I cut in?" like it was a perfectly reasonable request.

I backed away instinctively because girls at this age are terrifying and I looked at Derrick for some indication of what to do. He seemed uncertain, apologetic and delighted all at once. He shrugged, but in a compassionate way, and took her back into his arms.

I wandered off the dance floor alone and took a spot next to a kid named Daniel, who had been removed from the floor for groping. I looked at my shoes because I could not bear the sight of Derrick and Tabitha taking that last, infinitely significant dance to All-4-One. Daniel asked if I wanted to dance and for a moment I wondered if maybe I should just be more realistic about my station. I looked at him forlornly.

He added, ". . . But only if you're not wearing a bra."

Puberty is awful. Everything is confusing, painful and imbued with meaning. Others' opinions are of paramount importance and friendships can be established and obliterated in the span of a few hours. I took my status as a social pariah and parlayed it into ambition to be better, to show everyone that I wasn't worthless. Someday, I said to myself, none of these people will matter because I'm going to write the great American novel. I'm going to write serious literary fiction and win awards and people are going to care about my opinions and I'll be validated. Then I learned that when life hands you lemons, make dick jokes.

I don't look back on Derrick as my first love so much as the first flare of hormones that scrambled my brain and made me feel terrible feelings I could not control. Though I am strangely protective of the song if I hear it in a gym or candle store and those feelings still unfold as it plays.

Also, in high school, I went to a production of *Hair*, which happened to feature Tabitha. By that age I'd collected a few friends, and one of them was in it, so I sat in the front row to show support. During the big opening number, before Tabitha was to belt "When the mooooooooooon . . . ," she came out on stage and all these terrible memories flooded back. Going to performances like these gives me intense anxiety and I'm overtaken by a bizarre compulsion to interrupt them (to this day), so I was already volatile. Just as she opened her mouth, I threw a box of Thin Mints and hit her on the forehead, subsequently ruining the opening number.

I don't know why I did this. I don't like Thin Mints. I don't even know how I got them. Though this led to a forcible ejection from the auditorium, it was not the most unpleasant forcible ejection I have experienced and I still feel there should be no hard feelings, Tabitha, as long as Derrick and I can have our song.

THE MAN WHO FORGED A DILDO IN HIS OWN IMAGE

One of the worst people I've ever known was a young man who managed a small coffee shop in my hometown. We'll call him Coffee Thomas. He was the sort of person who, in conversation, even if you kept an invisible one-foot ring of space around you at all times, made you feel as though you were being molested. I guess that's insensitive to people who've actually been molested, so let's say it was *almost* like being molested. He was the sort of person concerned only with sex, much in the way that fraternity brothers and married academics tend to be, but Coffee Thomas did it with an air of sanctimony that only a privileged well-educated Northern Californian can impart. Sex is better, apparently, when you wake up with an agenda.

He was about average height, let's say five-foot-ten,

very bony and pale. He had dark brown eyes and very thick eyelashes—even attractively thick eyelashes—but you couldn't really appreciate anything on the top half of his face because it was always in competition with this smug, awful, self-impressed, shit-eating grin that never went away. Below the chin, his legs looked like bleached toothpicks that had been rolled around in brittle black hair for a while, which I know because he wore shorts, which is enough to question whether or not you should take any man seriously.

In this small town where I grew up in Northern California, Coffee Thomas's place of business was home to the only decent cup of coffee inside the city limits. Good coffee was important to me when I was a teenager because my identity was wholly subsumed by a desire for people to think I was an "intellectual," and my dull, primitive grasp of adult sophistication ended at "smart people take coffee very seriously, and thus so do I." Because of my vanity, I had no choice but to interact with Coffee Thomas.

Our parents knew each other to some degree, enough to be pleased that we were close enough in age to talk to each other and be friends. I'm fairly certain that parents in small towns are pleased by things like this because there is nothing else. In small towns like mine, there are effectively two restaurants and television. That's all. Naturally, one relishes trivialities like, "Hey, that thing we made a few years ago is approximately the same age as the Johnsons' thing and now they're talking to each other. Isn't that amazing?" It's not, but you take what you can get.

I started getting to know Coffee Thomas when I was

fourteen and he was eighteen. Then he was still a virgin and quite gawky and unattractive, but had that special breed of ego you get from being encouraged too much. Even at eighteen years old, ostrichlike and a virgin— virtually the most suffocating powerlessness a human being can experience—Coffee Thomas was still a total dick. He spent most of our limited conversations bragging about how he could "hack" my GeoCities account if he wanted and somehow aggressively alter my crude, pathetic, weird little webpage that no one but me knew about. I'd think nothing of his threats, buy my coffees and return home to gild Yoda Grrrl's Totally Awesome *Star Wars* webpage with more excellent MIDIs.

Something changed in Coffee Thomas right about the age he started having sex. I don't know the exact circumstances of this first dark, uncertain encounter in some bedroom far away. My guess is that a girl who felt equally powerless in life came to buy coffee one day and pitied him when she observed his leafing through *Gravity's Rainbow,* which he alluded to constantly in conversation despite never making it past the first ten pages. I know this for a fact because he would tell me things about the book and its greatness strictly in terms of what you could glean from its jacket. For example, he'd say, "It's a tremendous novel. It has something like a hundred and twenty central characters" but he couldn't really name any or tell you much about what they did. Anyway, I'm betting some teenage girl wanted to lose her own virginity and decided he was sexually nonthreatening enough to make it happen in a way that wouldn't scar her permanently. In the scenario I have crafted in my brain, there follow a few minutes of vociferous reaming and exactly one orgasm.

In the small, liberal enclave in Northern California where I grew up, you meet a lot of self-satisfied, unconsciously elitist liberals (like myself) who somehow support the town's astounding number of glass blowers, hemp boutiques and crystal shops. Coffee Thomas, being a shitty by-product of his New Agey environs, discovered "lovemaking" and, almost overnight, he was convinced that sex owed him because he was advancing it so swiftly.

Tangentially, the use of the word "lovemaking" is a terrific example of things horrible people say. In fact, it is almost impossible to talk about sex in slang or shorthand of any kind without being insufferable. All euphemisms for sex, with the exception of "having sex" or "fucking," are unacceptable. That includes "lovemaking," "doing it" and/or "the deed," "humping," "bumping uglies," "banging" and so on. All are horrible. This rule extends to body parts. "Breasts" is acceptable; "boobies," "cans," "funbags" and "sweater puppies" are not. "Penis" is acceptable, as well as "cock," but "shlong," "wang," "trouser snake," "member," "pecker," "piss weasel," "yogurt slinger" and/or "custard launcher," "johnson," "third leg," "babymaker," "sweetbreads" and "pink oboe" are not. Further still, do not describe things of which you approve as "sexy." Do not describe yourself or others as "horny" under any circumstances, as it is quite possibly the most awful word in the English language. Do not try to dress up the sex act as something that isn't completely filthy and perverse by calling it "lovemaking," and do not try to detract from its greatness by referring to it as "action." Every single one of these terms is "fundamentally sad." Honestly, the entire lexicon of sex and sexuality is deplorable and we'd really all do well to never talk about sex ever because all the words for it are ignoble. Please do not point out the irony of my proposing such a thing as the author of a collection of essays about sex. This heart isn't made of stone.

Let us not speculate too much on the origin of the hardening of Coffee Thomas's eerily joyless grin, and let's just say what needs to be said: Coffee Thomas started fucking homely girls left and right, and pretty soon he was fucking a different one every evening. His tastes tended toward "available." If I had to describe any evidence of his preference beyond willingness, I would say "older," "tragically grateful," a proclivity for "beaded shirts," having a notable "smell of chickpeas," owning "several incense burners" and being "fundamentally sad."

Where it used to be that I suffered through only a few minutes of nerdy, baseless threats, buying coffee soon become a gauntlet. I'd approach the shop, he'd put down that week's postmodern literature or Eastern philosophy he was pretending to read, and say, "Guess what?" And so it began that while he made me coffee, I listened to what last night's woman was open to do with his penis.

She was always a model. Or should have been. She was always "unbelievably gorgeous," tall and thin and all the other markers for conventional beauty. Then, because it was a small town, my family would be seated across the room from him at our town's one Japanese restaurant and I'd watch him lecture neighboring tables that sushi is eaten with the hands in order to impress his date . . . a forty-something frizzy-haired aspiring jewelry designer who had taken up belly dancing to find herself.

I found him repugnant. I stopped going there for coffee. I started making it at home.

My parents kept going to the coffee shop and Coffee Thomas shared tell of his conquests with my father in the same terrible candor but refrained from doing so with my mother, so neither of them had any reason to dislike him. One of them must have expressed that my absence had to do with hurt feelings and I guess Coffee Thomas didn't want that. A few months after I disappeared from his coffee shop—I was about fifteen at the time—he sent a message through my father that he'd like to bury the hatchet. My father gave him our home number, which he called. He got me on the phone and invited me out for tacos. I was cornered, and my parents had whatever weird stake they did in wanting me and him to be friends, so I agreed.

He picked me up in his car and we drove to a local Mexican restaurant. We ordered at the counter and sat down; we hadn't said very much to each other beyond the usual pleasantries that people exchange. I should have taken this to mean that we had nothing in common, shared no sensibilities or interests or preferences and had absolutely no reason to stage this impersonation of friendship for our parents. There was no loss here in our not being friends! There was no point for us to patch anything up because we weren't working with anything that could be fixed. No hard feelings; let's go back to our respective homes.

We got our food and started to try our hand at conversa-

tion and, because he's horrible, he immediately started criticizing my eating habits. Granted, I eat like I should be wearing
a helmet when I'm unsupervised, but he said to me, "You
know, you'd be a lot healthier if you slowed down to actually
enjoy what you're eating."

This seemed silly because the only rational explanation
for why I eat the way I do is that I enjoy it too much. "What?"

Coffee Thomas's way was that of superiority and he leaned
back in his chair with much satisfaction and said, "Chew your
drink, and drink your food, that's what I believe," then he
looked at me deeply, as if tedium at the dinner table was the
gateway to nirvana.

Conversation started and stopped like this for a few minutes, until I became resigned to sit there and eat my tacos in
uneasy silence. Because Coffee Thomas could not resist being listened to, he abhorred silence. Apparently unable to
stop himself, he pointed to a woman seated across the restaurant and said, "See her?" and I nodded because my eyeballs
work, "I took her out a few weeks ago. Isn't she beautiful?"
He waved to her and she looked away mortified because she
was seated with what appeared to be her husband and
children.

Maybe Coffee Thomas was just on a higher plane than
me, like he believed he was. Maybe he was less judgmental
and more receptive and loving and giving, and maybe he saw
beauty with eyes that were just more open than mine (despite
their workmanlike effectiveness). But no, she was not. She
was emphatically not. She was a regular-looking lady, if not
particularly mousy, who thought nothing of fucking a teenager despite her marriage.

I was unsettled. "No."

"You're wrong," he said. Then he paused and added, "Besides, you'd really have to see her with her clothes off to know how beautiful she is."

"Dude. That is exactly what I'm talking about."

"What do you mean?"

"That's gross."

"There's nothing gross about what she and I are capable of together."

"No, that's not what I'm saying. All you do is talk about your sex life, even though I don't care and I find it off-putting. I also think it's completely gross and tasteless to point out women you've slept with. That's not my business and it's not yours to make it mine."

"You know what your problem is?"

"No."

"You're a prude."

"What? No, I'm not."

"Yes, you are. What I'm talking about—what I live—is not only a part of life, it's the most beautiful part of life. It's an expression of everything that elevates us. It's physical enlightenment. And you don't realize that and you try to apply your Judeo-Christian morality to it, but it's completely outside of that."

As surprising as it was—for the first time in my life—to be accused of being too Judeo-Christian in my morals, I don't take kindly to being yelled at in restaurants by my contemporaries. I told him, "This is outside a discussion of my morality. I think it's inappropriate and gross for you to constantly brag about all the sex you have."

Coffee Thomas looked at me for a long serious moment and said, "I've never had sex."

Then he paused and let me hope against hope it had all been a big, strange, meaningless dream. A hallucination.

". . . But I've made love about a thousand times."

"That's it." I stood up and told him it was time to go home. He reminded me that we'd taken his car to get there and unless I wanted to walk the whole way, I was at his mercy. I told him that if he didn't take me home, I would call my parents and tell them I couldn't stand the sight of his face anymore. Sensing the social embarrassment of having to involve parents, he agreed to take me home. I gathered up my uneaten dinner in a takeout container and we walked silently to his Subaru Outback (obviously) in the parking lot. Once inside, things went really wrong.

As I said, he was not a fan of silence, but there was no hoping we might have a conversation with any civility anymore. He said he had some CDs in the glove compartment and asked, through his teeth, if I could suffer long enough to do him the small favor of picking one out. I had no objection to spending the next ten minutes listening to music instead of his self-content, so I opened the glove compartment.

Out tumbled a translucent purple dildo.

It landed in my lap and writhed there like a newborn worm. I looked at it.

There are times in life when things happen that are so outside the bounds of reality and acceptable occurrence that you're unable to process them and so instead regard their unfolding with a kind of emotionless distance.

When its writhing stopped and the dildo was still between my knees, I said, "Why the fuck do you have a dildo in your glove compartment?"

"Relax," he said, "It's me."

"What?"

"It's me. I had it made."

"I don't—" I didn't! "What do you mean?"

"It's me. It's a silicone mold of my penis."

"What—"

"I met this girl, she's unbelievably beautiful . . ."

"Oh my God."

"But I'm going away next week and I want her to enjoy me when I'm not around."

"Stop the car. Stop the fucking car right now."

"Calm down, it's not like it's been used yet—"

"Now."

The Outback came to an abrupt stop along the road. I gingerly used my takeout container's brown paper bag to remove the dildo from its place on my lap and then I tossed it at him, because you only get so many opportunities in life to use a dildo offensively. I then opened the passenger's side door, got out and walked the rest of the way home. We have not spoken since.

Looking back, what strikes me most about this waking nightmare is that his behavior seemed to suggest I should be less appalled because the dildo was really just a big glittery Xerox of his own cock. Had a garden-variety dildo landed in my lap, would my shock have been warranted? It seemed I should have been soothed to know that the dildo was just a fleshy raincheck for his weird peen.

To this day, I'm uncertain why that would affect whether or not this thing surpassed a social boundary, but I've never made a dick joke quite the same again. If I learned any lasting lessons, it's to remain wary of glove compartments and refuse to open them if such a request is made. Further, I even struggle sometimes to enjoy tacos, which—frankly—hurts the most.

THE TIME I ATTENDED AN ORGY

I was a pretty late bloomer when it came to boys. Most girls started holding hands in third or fourth grade, kissing in fifth or sixth, dry humping—as teens are wont—by eighth. Because my hometown was so small, most of the kids with whom I attended kindergarten ended up right alongside me in high school. Consequently, if you'd forged a reputation as chubby and unlikeable in elementary school, it was pretty hard to shake.

I ended up getting my first kiss at fifteen when I went to visit a friend in rural Maine and got to be the exciting new girl for a few weeks. I was Californian and blond enough so they were all really impressed at how I wore sunglasses even when it was overcast and they asked me if I knew any movie stars. That first kiss came from a young aspiring pharmacist who was a foot shorter than me and had tricked out his car to look like KITT from *Knight Rider*. He was a nice guy. My second kiss was from an older boy with a devilock, so that's one I can be proud of.

My already slow development was further stymied by isolation due to homeschooling, which I'd taken up in seventh grade. As soon as you take a moment to breathe that out and let your shock subside, I'll say that I started homeschooling for reasons that are neither relevant nor terribly interesting. The point is I ended up in a charter school program that had me taking classes at the local community college, which was terrifying after a few years of schooling alone.

I was socially inept and disinterested in dating of any kind until the first day of my sociology course, when this guy walked in and obliterated all solitary impulse: he was wolfishly handsome with straight black hair cut in a perfect rock 'n' roll shag. Of course, he dressed like a sexually aggressive eleven-year-old at a mall goth store in baggy jeans and bowling shirts and he had a wallet chain. I know I've already mentioned that teenage hormones can make you discard reason, but it's quite remarkable just how fully they can make you discard taste as well.

I stared at him throughout that entire first class and could not believe his cheekbones. It was a real infatuation at first sight and one that persisted even when he spoke. The first time I heard his voice was when our extremely urbane German sociology professor was tasked with answering a stupid question about evolution. He mentioned, offhand, the lemur.

"Oh yeah!" the beautiful one exclaimed, "Like aye-ayes."

"Pardon me?" said the professor.

"Like those aye-aye things in Madagascar. Natives kill them because they think they're, like, demons."

The professor looked at him silently, straightened his

glasses and returned to talking about real things. In retrospect, this interaction revealed nothing appealing about him, but at the time I sat there in class drawing hearts on my notepad as my own swelled with thoughts of *He likes animals!* In this way, teenage girls have no survival skills and are unequipped for the world.

For the rest of the semester, I'd stare at him longingly through class and think of him around the clock. It was silly because I knew I'd never work up the confidence to speak with him myself. Or anyone. I knew no one else in the class and spoke to no one else on campus. I'd show up, attend my classes, go home and quietly do my homework. Every day.

As the semester progressed, I noticed a few of the more sexually advanced girls (all of them nineteen or twenty) would talk to him after class. To this day, I always get kind of jealous of women who can sit on desks and make it look so insouciant and enticing and effortless and it's exactly thoughts like these that make me the sort of person who cannot sit insouciantly on a fucking desk.

One such girl ended up sitting next to me in class one day. A few minutes before class began, I took off my sunglasses and slid them into their case. She caught the designer logo labeled inside and looked at me startled, as if the weird, un-likeable lump of matter beside her had suddenly become sentient and interesting. Little did she know I'd gotten them from an outlet mall.

"Great glasses," she said in that slow, contralto, drawn-out way that sexually advanced teenage girls do so well. "I'm looking for a new pair. I lost mine over spring break."

I was really frightened that this girl was talking to me,

because she wore hoop earrings and tight pants. I looked at her with wide eyes and she must have interpreted this as awe, because she continued.

"Yeah, I was down in TJ, partying like a rock star."

"Oh," I said and I had absolutely no idea where that was. Tangentially, I did not crack the code that LA and Los Angeles were the same place until high school.

"Yeah," she said and grinned coyly, "my nose still hurts."

"Did you fall on it?"

She paused for a moment and looked at me unsurely. Then she laughed. "You're funny. What's your name?"

Her name was Tiffany. Before long, she started sitting next to me in class and asking me questions about homework. Soon after, some of her other attractive friends started to sit in little satellite formations around us. They were all cooler and older and sexually experienced and carried themselves as such. I was waiting for them to figure out I was sixteen and a virgin and slept with the lights on. Or that I maintained a scrapbook filled with pictures of my favorite action figures. Or that I drew portraits of myself eating spaghetti with Dostoevsky, one noodle strung between our lips like in *Lady and the Tramp*. Or that I was wearing Batman underwear from the little boys' section of JC Penney. Or that I'd spent my last two months' worth of Saturday nights *making a suit of chain mail*.

One day after class, Tiffany came up to me and asked what I was doing later that night. I told her I didn't have any plans and she said some of her friends from class were organizing a study session at her place. The midterm was about two weeks off and our professor's tests were notoriously hard, so I agreed.

She motioned to the tall, beautiful teenage boy. "We're going to study with him."

I tried not to show the thrill in my spine and shrugged. "Cool," I said. *Just like in the movies!*

"It'll be really fun," Tiffany continued, "four girls and one guy," and it was here she offered an exaggerated, cartoonish wink. She gave me directions to her place and told me to show up around eight, which I thought was pretty late to start studying, but I figured she was so popular she must have lots of social engagements to attend after school or had to buy more hoop earrings and cutoffs.

I went home and ritualistically showered, slathered myself in the nicest moisturizers I owned and meticulously obscured my face in cosmetics. I made a bunch of flash cards from the text we'd been studying because I figured men were impressed by fastidiousness. Then I sat back and stared at the ceiling and wondered what it would be like to finally talk to him. I told my parents where I was off to and left half an hour before eight because I am chronically early to everything. I figured that punctuality, in addition to prim organization, would make me irresistible.

I was the first one at Tiffany's apartment, which was the kind of space you fantasize about when you're a teenager living with your parents: a windowless basement in someone else's house with low ceilings and no stove. She let me in and asked if I'd like some Turkish coffee, which I found supremely exotic.

I cataloged every object in her apartment, awed at what it was like to be an adult and independent and capricious and cook things with a hot plate. She had a print of *Starry Night* taped to her wall. All other decorative art came in the form of—I'm serious—framed vanity shots of herself. One whole wall was just a bunch of black-and-white headshots, arty portraits, candid photos of her smiling with her eyes closed or being held up in a bikini on the beach by a row of interchangeable ripped dudes. There was even a painting of her with a sheet slipping down to reveal her breasts. She came over to me looking at all the photos and handed me an espresso cup.

"I used to model," she said.

I was so out of my league. "Why'd you stop?"

"They kept telling me my legs were too long."

I nodded with intense admiration.

"They want girls to look perfect but not, you know, like *too perfect*," she said and shrugged with all the wisdom and experience one could have in life.

I remember thinking that even with an age difference of three years, she seemed infinitely older than me. I wanted her to teach me to be like her. I wanted to sleep on a mattress on the floor in a windowless basement and demonstrate my cursory knowledge of art history and decorate with glamour shots of myself and steal perfume from the mall. I wanted to have to walk through someone else's living room to take a shower. And then.

"So," she said, looking contemplatively at one of the photos of herself as I wondered at the vastness of her thoughts, "let me take your bag."

I handed her my backpack, weighed down with textbooks and flash cards and binders and even a stapler because you never know, etc.

She looked momentarily confused. "Did you bring toys?"

I looked at her and recalled that our entire interaction since the beginning had been a delicate series of facial expressions indicating I knew what she was talking about when I absolutely did not. I considered for a moment and concluded there was no way to fake this one. "Pardon?"

"Yeah," she said as if it were obvious, "vibrators, dildos, anal beads, handcuffs?"

". . . What?"

She grinned from ear to ear. "I told you we were going to *study* with that guy from class. You didn't think I meant we were going to actually, like, read textbooks, right?"

"No! No, of course not," by which I meant, *I've never even seen my own vagina.* I laughed extra long to buy some time. I could hear my heart beating between my ears. *They were going to have sex with him! All at once! With me.* The only thing more terrifying than losing your virginity in front of older, hotter people seemed like being the prude who declines the orgy because it's a school night. What the fuck was I going to do? I fumbled. I worried. Time was running out. I laughed again, feigning more nervousness. ". . . I've just never used handcuffs." Oh, me.

She lit up. "We'll fix that. They can be really fun. So," she held up the backpack again, "did you bring anything?"

I nodded frantically. "Yeah, totally. I have, like . . . four . . . anal beads in there."

She looked confused, lifting the bulging pack and shaking it, trying to determine how it could be so heavy.

I nodded urgently. "They're huge."

Her eyes widened. "Kinky," she said with the kind of witless, automatic approval of the unfathomable that had been my de facto response for the entirety of our time together. It was then her phone began to ring and she walked off. "That's probably the other girls . . ."

By myself for the moment, the panic really set in. I had no idea how I was going to get out of this without seeming relentlessly prudish and un-fun and therefore, worse still, unfuckable. Not to mention, at that age I watched porn because I thought it was hilarious, had never masturbated and thought you could get an orgasm from kissing.

Then, of course, he showed up. She was on the phone and let him in. He came over to where I was and introduced himself. The thrill of actually touching his hand was almost too much to bear, considering it felt like my vital organs were all shutting down in unison. He was so much taller than me. He then set his backpack down and it landed heavily. There was hope for me yet.

"What'd you bring?" I asked.

He looked at me oddly and said, "The textbook?"

"Me, too!" I blurted.

". . . Cool," he said, nodding unsurely. He went to sit down.

I turned my attention to Tiffany's phone conversation going on in the kitchen. "What do you mean you can't get it?" she was saying. "We need like a gram. I don't fucking care what his deal is." Her face crinkled. "Then go get some more."

There I was in the basement with my knees bent so my head didn't touch the ceiling, wondering how I was going to talk my way out of this weeknight teenage orgy and the four supposedly enormous anal beads in my backpack without sounding like the child I absolutely was. Some sort of rash flaring up out of nowhere? No, that would ruin future sexual appeal. I didn't have any condoms! No, that didn't seem to deter teenagers any from fucking. It's not like they teach you to prepare for this. Hours before I'd been making flash cards about social stratification and then *bam!* The boy I've loved from afar for months is going to handcuff me and take my virginity in a moldy basement while a former model watches beneath a frayed poster of *Starry Night.*

I looked around and saw him sitting quietly, staring off into space, and the room seemed to go quiet and I realized the only way out of this was to tell the truth. If he didn't like me anymore because I was a socially inept, frightened virgin who didn't want to have group sex with him, then we just weren't meant to be. I was going to tell them the truth and if that was embarrassing or objectionable to them, then they could fuck off and I was more than happy to go home right then and complete the best damn suit of chain mail Wine Country had ever seen. So I stood up and started to shake.

"I'm really sorry," I began.

He looked at me, uncertain.

"Motherfucker!" Tiffany shouted. She stormed into the living room and said, "Their fucking car just broke down and the fucking dealer is getting paranoid. I need to go bail these bitches out, so you guys have to go. Let's take a raincheck."

It was like my fever broke. I grabbed my backpack and dashed out the front door without saying goodbye to either of them. I made it to the Volvo my mother had loaned me for the night, trying to unlock the driver's side door as fast as possible. I dropped the keys in the dirt, shouted a stream of expletives and knelt down to find them. While I frantically searched,

Tiffany hurried outside and drove away. He came outside, too. He went to his own car, stopped, walked back around and stood over me.

"What's with you?" he asked.

"They were going to have sex with you," I said, now more anguished by the missing car keys than anything that had transpired before.

"Those girls?"

"Yeah. They said it was going to be a study session but I guess that means orgy. How am I supposed to know that? I'm a homeschooler."

I found the keys just as he walked back to his car and sat down on the hood. I stood up and, for some reason, had the idea to walk over to him.

"I kind of thought that's what was going on," he said, "but you can never be too careful, so I brought the textbook and a box of condoms."

I sat down next to him. "I guess that's pretty smart."

"Community college girls are all about the dick," he said. I thought he, too, sounded very worldly.

I sighed and shrugged and at this point, the whole harrowing ordeal had subsided and my nerves were left to fray and I had no more will to fret about my desirableness. "I wouldn't know."

He squinted at me. "You're weird. How old are you?"

"Not old enough for this."

He laughed and I lit a cigarette and he made fun of me for not being old enough for that, either. We sat on the hood of his car for a while and talked about all the things we had in common, which were actually very few. Having just one TV show you both watched growing up or reading the same book and liking it seems like all the intimacy in the universe when you're sixteen.

I'm still pretty proud of myself for being ready to stick to my guns like that and turn down an orgy with the best-looking person I'd ever seen. He and I became friends and started dating about six months later. When I eventually lost my virginity to him on a twin bed in an equally filthy house he shared with an obsessive-compulsive forty-five-year-old Scientologist who refused to throw away newspapers, I remember looking up at the ceiling as the Internet radio "chill" drum and bass played and having no idea I was about to be in the worst relationship of my life. So, if you think about it, sticking to my guns that time really fucked me.

SEXUAL PREDATORS AND ME

In the six months between avoiding that orgy and when I actually lost my virginity, I had another occasion to lose it and I'm extremely glad I opted not to. After the orgy situation, I resigned myself to not being sophisticated enough for my male classmate (whom I'd eventually date) and, during this period of dejection, I met a man who was what I can call now, with some hindsight, a sexual predator. And by "with some hindsight," I mean "by applying critical thought."

When you're sixteen or seventeen, you have absolutely no clue what's good for you and what obviously isn't. You can be flattered, manipulated, charmed into believing just about anything or anyone. These generic statements are how I've decided to begin an extremely personal account of shitty decisions I made or nearly made as a teenager, and after that I'll try to step back and shoehorn you into my own experiences again somehow.

The junior college ended up giving me enough socialization that I eventually entered the time-honored teenage girl stage of dressing like a midrange escort. First, I threw out all my old clothes. Gone were the XXL Oasis tees in sherbet, replaced by bondage-y plaid skirts and visible garter straps and this weird Renaissance blouse that interlaced all the way down the front, to the navel. I'm not proud of this phase. At the time I thought I was very chic and provocative like an editorial in *W*, but really I just looked like an asshole and my bra was showing all the time. There I was, about sixteen—and a very young sixteen at that—now trying to direct male attention to me, where before I'd taken a very passive role in flirtation.

I had a friend named Craig, who was nineteen or so and didn't live with his parents. Craig was (and is) a fundamentally decent person and this story isn't about him. He worked in some technological capacity for the theater department at the local junior college. One night, a bunch of friends and I went to see a performance of *The Tempest* he was working on. We were all enjoying the play as much as you actually enjoy watching this caliber of Shakespeare production and then Ferdinand—sweet, boring, simple-brained Ferdinand—took the stage.

You're not supposed to like Ferdinand as a character because he's lame and one-dimensional, yet there I was transfixed. I don't recall much about his skills beyond that he was a little fey and overbearing but I do remember his face. He held himself like an adult. It turned out he was one.

After the performance, Craig and a bunch of his lighting friends were smoking on the steps of the theater. I was there, all tall and awkward, wearing some stupid long black coat. Ferdinand appeared in our circle and I was too excited and embarrassed to even speak. It wasn't so bad, actually, because I didn't think anything of myself at the time and so figured he wasn't interested in me anyway.

His name turned out to be Jesse and Jesse turned out to be Craig's new roommate. Jesse was also an astounding twenty-four years of age, mature beyond comprehension as far as I was concerned. He looked like Cary Elwes in *The Princess Bride*, but more sexually threatening (basically, perfect). Suddenly I wanted any and every excuse to hang out at Craig's house. It so happened that they were throwing a wrap party that weekend and I was invited. I went home that night and taped the playbill into my diary and wrote about Jesse's handsomeness.

That weekend at the party, I spent the first hour or so pretending to be cool. I was talking to Craig and other mutual friends, smoking, not making eye contact, talking loud enough to get Jesse's attention but seeming not to cultivate it any further. Then I went upstairs. Because I am *fucking mysterious.*

I had devised a plan. I had devised the dumbest plan ever imagined in the history of teenagers. I went upstairs and sat down in a room by myself and pulled out a notepad I'd brought. I began to scribble notes on it—meaningless ones, of course, but nebulously related to whatever unreadable novel I was working on at the time. My plan, of course, was to lure Jesse's attention by revealing myself as a fellow creative, so compelled by my instincts that I needed to slip away and channel the muse. There I sat, alone with a notepad, in tortured artist drag.

Wouldn't you know it, about half an hour later, just as I was considering giving up, Jesse wandered around the door. To my great joy, he appeared to have been looking for me. I was nearly too thrilled to speak when he sat down. Now I will relay some dialogue that agonizes me to see in print.

"What . . . are . . . you doing?" he asked with the flared pauses of a community college theater major, the question itself like an illicit dare. He tucked his chin when he spoke, so he always seemed to be peering at you from under his brow; a great trick in any young man's arsenal to make himself appear more complicated.

"Writing," I replied with all the importance in the world, for questions like his were meant for gilded answers. *Because that's what my soul wants.*

"Why?" he asked with sudden, obvious interest.

Here I mustered the kind of gravity and bottomless self-importance that only an overencouraged sixteen-year-old virgin can access and said, "Actors have to act," and I gestured to him languidly like a character in a foreign film or how I imagined that would go, "writers . . . have to write."

Look, I'm sorry. Clearly as a teenager I was the worst person on earth. However, I can handle sharing this exchange because no one who reads it would come off any better. As teenagers, we all made others endure our misguided and bottomless narcissism. Not every teenager affects these appalling pretensions exactly, but just about every teenager is an idiot. It's only a matter of what kind.

We discussed the extremely serious novel I was working

on and he talked about his aspirations as an actor/musician. As for his aspirations of being a sex offender, he kept that pretty close to the chest. We ended up talking for half an hour or so before Craig noted our absence and came upstairs to find us. Craig insisted we come back downstairs and I hated him for an instant. The rest of the night went on. Jesse ended up getting so drunk that we didn't talk to each other again.

Soon I was spending every afternoon and evening I could at Craig's, eking out any excuse to be there. If I was in the neighborhood, I'd stop by. I'd call and ask if Craig needed a lift or wanted to get dinner so we could hang out at his place after.

My parents noticed I was spending all my time away from home. At this point, those two rode a pretty hard line that I wasn't supposed to have sex until I could support myself financially (i.e., not under their roof). Still, robust conversation—and ruthless bluntness—are Cardiff family hallmarks.

I was sitting in the car one day with my father, shrewd and attentive, and he asked if there was anything they should know about. I told him that I was hanging out at Craig's and it was nothing like that. Because I am incapable of hiding things from my parents, the fuckers, I added that Craig had a handsome roommate, although that had nothing to do with my sudden disappearance.

Just to drive home how incapable I was of lying to them, I then blurted out that Craig's handsome roommate was twenty-four. There was a silence between my father and me. I realized I had overplayed the hand.

Theater. He's into theater.

"I think he's gay, though."

My father looked at me skeptically. At this point he'd already rooted out what was going on. "He's gay, huh?"

Wait. Don't say yes to that. Sudden visions of a perfect world flooded my dumb teen brain, visions of Jesse and me together and happy and standing on clouds and maybe a garland or some other flowy thing in my hair. How would my parents ever make the leap from Jesse being gay to Jesse being my fiancé? I needed to set expectations without startling them.

"Yeah. I mean, I think. I'm not sure. He's kind of asexual."

"Oh?"

"Yeah, I guess. Like, a regular guy but not . . . like . . . sleazy."

What. The. Fuck. Are. You. Saying.

"All right," my father said and nodded. "He's twenty-four?"

"Yes."

"You're sixteen."

And then I got that defensive teenage tone. "I know."

"So," my father said, "you can keep spending time at Craig's house. But if this guy touches you, I'm going to kill him with a bat."

Don't let the violence of that alarm you. This was my father's de facto response to hearing about boys. My parents were incredibly permissive and trusting of me all the time, but as soon as the subject of teenage sex was broached, my father became some sort of barbarian conquerer, braining his enemies on the temple steps with savage precision. It was pretty endearing.

Though I had kind of blown my cover, it didn't matter because I wasn't banned from Craig's. I was free to explore this thing with Jesse as I saw fit.

Days went on, and the more time I spent at Craig's apartment, the more I became exposed to Jesse's eccentricities. When you're a teenager in a small town in California and the only things that make you feel less alone are Marc Bolan and *The Simpsons*, you are pretty vulnerable to the appeal of eccentricities in charming, handsome older men.

Shows? He likes watching shows? And listening to music?!

For one, Jesse was obsessed with Bruce Lee, which is a pretty cool obsession to have. He kept in shape by practicing Jeet Kune Do in his room while listening to electronica. If that doesn't turn you on, you are probably not a sixteen-year-old girl. He had even (seemingly) read books. Most alluring of all, he talked openly and explicitly about sex, in a manner that teenage boys I knew were incapable of doing. Once he left a tie on the coffee table and I picked it up and he chuckled to himself that he'd tied an ex-girlfriend to his bed with it and then "went down on her."

As an adult, I know that offering this kind of information, solicited or otherwise, is objectionable. As a teenager, I found it provocative—though Coffee Thomas did more or less the exact same thing, he didn't have the smoldering good looks or self-possessedness of Jesse. I also didn't consider the dubious logistics of the statement, what with his bed being a mattress on the floor. I spent longer, later nights there, just wanting Jesse to talk to me and pay attention to me and invite me a little bit deeper into his strange world of adulthood.

Then one day, Craig had to run a sudden errand and Jesse and I were left alone.

Jesse asked me if I'd heard of some obscure post-grunge band and I was completely amazed because I! Had! Not! He put on the CD and I wasn't into it but it was still exciting that he knew about music I didn't. We sat there on opposite ends of the living room, as I fidgeted nervously in my polyester adult costume strung together from mall stores and the space between us got smaller and smaller.

It had to start somewhere. He started it. And so: "Does it bother you that I'm twenty-four?"

There is no way to answer a question like that when you're in such a situation. I froze where I sat and waited for my heart to slow down. He was finally naming the unspoken thing, finally remarking on all the tension that had transpired for what felt like ages but was actually about a week and a half.

I could do this. ". . . No."

In that exact moment, his expression went from this silly cultivated artist's incredulity to what can only be described as *tractor beam fuck eyes*. He said, "It doesn't bother me either." He might as well have added a patronizing "Do you understand?"

On the inside, I was screaming, *Of course it doesn't bother me! Obviously it doesn't bother me! Can't you tell? There's no conflict here!* Moreover, the subject of our age difference was a perverse thrill. How, then, to keep the conversation going?

I started to feel a little bit the provocateur myself. "Why not?"

His gaze didn't waver. "I'm not going to let someone I've never met tell me how I can or can't feel. I'm not going to live my life by some law in a book somewhere. Some book I'll never read."

If alarms are going off in your head, it's because you've spotted a sexual predator. Some teenage girls, unfortunately, do not recognize these signs. Notice how he deceptively couched this statement in a language of having "controversial feelings" as opposed to simply "wanting to fuck an impressionable young girl."

He continued, "I shouldn't be penalized because of some antiquated, puritanical beliefs. We shouldn't be penalized. It's not our fault this country is so repressed. I'm not repressed. I"—and the gaze lingered over the rest of me—"don't think you are either."

I stared at him blankly and was still as stone in my mall clothes. I would probably agree to anything he said I was.

"We could go," he said, alighting on that old trope of the romance in fleeing together, "we could go to France." For lack of *originalité*.

My knowledge of France at sixteen was informed entirely by the chef in *The Little Mermaid*. Despite that, I suddenly wanted to go to France. Additionally, I wanted to be with someone who wanted to go to France, who had reason to think France was a good place to go. Pretty much everything about France suddenly seemed amazing.

"Can you imagine?" he said and he paused dramatically and let that stare land back on my face and linger for a while and then he outright said it and it still floors me to this day: "Fucking in Paris?"

I was transported. There we were, postcoital in whatever limited way I understood that to look like, endlessly adult, beautiful and sweaty. Age, nothing but a number. Baskets of baguettes and croissants in the foreground, room service. Satin sheets. Every curtain, carpet and comforter a riot of flowers, as I apparently believed the French were partial to loud floral prints. We lay in a bed in a beautiful expansive room in the most magnificent hotel in Paris: the Eiffel Tower.

I nodded. I could totally imagine "fucking in Paris." Again, mind you, I did not understand the actual "fucking" part or Paris, as both still confused and terrified me. But I could vaguely grasp the idea of it. The liberty of our encounter, unencumbered by American law. I didn't want to be repressed! I wanted to reject repression! The French just got it. They didn't care if you fucked children.

He closed the gap between us and was beside me on the couch, hovering near my face, engaged in a sudden hilarious pantomime of inward struggle. He wanted to kiss me but he could not! Because of Puritans or whatever! (Sorry, by the way, but all feelings as a teenager are accompanied by exclamation points.)

Suddenly he was over me, putting his lips almost to mine, wincing visibly and pulling away. This was so hard for him! It was wrong! He didn't want to be right! This was the last moment for a little while that I would exercise some good judgment, because I recalled finding the whole display so genuinely silly that I became embarrassed for him and kissed him so he would stop.

This was not my first kiss, but it was the first I remember indelibly. It was electric and thrilling and strange. Something I perceived as passionate, but for him was something else. He was older and experienced and was a man with a man's body and I knew that because he wore a tank top. Just as the excitement began to sweep all reason away, the front door swung open and Craig walked in. He burst out laughing and ran back outside. Jesse sprang up and ran after him. I found them faux wrestling in the front yard—which is a weirdly common response young men have to things that make them uncomfortable. The whole thing was so weird that no one really said anything, they just giggled uncontrollably and wrestled. Which proved, of course, that everyone involved was adult enough for love and sex and Paris.

I hung out for another hour or two and Craig made fun of us a lot. When it was time for me to go, Jesse walked me to my car and kissed me again. I drove home that night wondering if I was in love with him because this is how hormones work when you are sixteen and fucking dumb. This is also the part where I wish someone could have explained to me what was happening.

The next week, my time at Craig's didn't abate any; I just spent it differently. Jesse and I made out breathlessly in his room. We'd stop suddenly at my insistence and start talking about our age difference. We talked frankly and endlessly about my virginity and how he'd like to take it. He presented himself as someone who could show me a world I didn't know existed. Then we'd make out some more.

For the time, I was stopping things whenever they began to challenge the bounds of typical teenage heavy petting. The world of men was still frightening and bizarre to me and I needed to know that I was making the right decision. He was respectful enough when I wouldn't let things go very far but his aggravation seemed to increase every time I drew his hands away.

It was those conversations that kind of haunt me. The substance of all of them was that I was so much more than a teenager to him, that I was more perceptive and thoughtful than even his peers, that I was funnier and my interests were cool and adult like his own. I liked glam-rock and Westerns and post-punk and Russian literature. He flattered me, he coaxed me to believe that at sixteen I was more worldly than any woman he knew . . . except in one specific way. He wanted to be the man to change that.

When I drove home at night, I would be alone on the highway, trying to meet my self-imposed midnight curfew. I would drive the whole way noiselessly mouthing over and over that I was in love with him. For some reason, though, I couldn't bring myself to let anything happen between us. This is what I am now able to identify as a bit of miraculous self-preservation instinct, one of the few times in my life such a thing has ever reared its bland, prudent head.

One night, about two weeks after our initial kiss, I showed up for a party at the apartment and Jesse was drunk in the front yard, unable to stand. At least, I thought he was drunk. He'd fallen and his nose was bleeding. He paid no attention to me that night. I ended up crashing on the couch. The next morning, he was gone and I felt strangely rejected. I didn't understand why he hadn't waited for me. I didn't understand why he hadn't paid attention to me the night before.

I was on the couch, bleary-eyed and puzzled when Craig came downstairs.

"Where's Jesse?" I asked.

"Good morning to you, too," he said.

"Sorry."

"He went to school to work on some music course assignment." He looked annoyed.

"Oh." I looked down and wondered why he hadn't woken me up to say good morning or goodbye or validate my maturity in that enormously gratifying way. "Thanks for letting me crash last night."

"Yeah," Craig said and his delivery was uncharacteristically clipped, "hopefully it's going to be the last party we have for a while." He sauntered out into their small backyard and I watched him through the sliding glass doors as he began picking up the night's empty bottles of cheap beer.

I got up and followed him outside. "What's with you?"

"Nothing."

I stepped out onto the cold brick in the backyard and watched him fling bottles into a trash bag. I knew an edge when I saw one. "Seriously. What's going on?"

He looked up at me and scowled. "Well, Jesse keeps having parties and not cleaning up any of the shit." He motioned to a pile of two or three enormous trash bags bulging with bottles of cheap beer. "You think he cleaned those up?"

I immediately searched for some defense. "He's got a lot of schoolwork."

"You mean his Introduction to Music Composition course? Which isn't worth any credits? He dropped everything else but that and the play."

"Oh."

"But he's still acting like he doesn't have time to get a job."

Craig paused and looked at me and I could see he was debating internally. After another moment he said, "And he can't pay utilities but somehow he can always score coke."

"Coke?"

My small Northern California town was endlessly permissive of a specific strain of drug culture: marijuana was not so much ubiquitous as it was practically forced on you, while hallucinogenic mushrooms were widely available (if not encouraged) and LSD considered of a kind. These drugs promised to make you better understand yourself and the universe and inner workings of things and make you tolerate reggae and what have you, drugs I never tried growing up because I paid too much attention when my friends got high. So-called "hard drugs," though, were demonized there like everywhere else, if not a little more because of their unnatural aspect. Cocaine was what movie villains did, as far as I knew, and movie villains didn't care how their produce was sourced.

"Yeah." A bottle shattered on the bricks. Craig let out a loud exasperated sigh, leaned over and started gathering up the glass.

"Jesse does coke?"

"You haven't noticed? He does coke all the time. His nose was bleeding all over the place last night."

"He fell."

"No, he 'lost equilibrium,' according to him. According to me he was drunk and coked up and tripped on a bush."

The idea of Jesse high on coke and falling into a topiary in their front yard was inconsistent with my romantic fantasies. He was measured, masculine, adult. Finding out the embodiment of maturity you've convinced yourself you love is kind of a fuck-up was like finding out the Giving Tree ate children. I was astonished. I refused to believe it could be true.

"Ashley," Craig said, "I know you have a crush on him and everything, but have you noticed that he's a complete scumbag?"

"No, he's not," I insisted. I was in love with him.

"Yes, he fucking is. Do you think you're the first sixteen-year-old girl he's brought around?"

That stopped me.

"It was the same thing with a different one a couple weeks ago. Counting you, there's been three since I've known him. Like, in the couple months he's lived here."

"They were sixteen, too?"

"Yeah," and he emptied an ashtray bloated with wet cigarette butts into the bag, "one of them had just turned sixteen." He returned to the scattered pieces of the broken bottle.

There was no real way to harness that particular drowning sensation of outrage and heartbreak. Not only was it devastating to realize all at once that he'd been lying to me—making me feel special and mature and somehow miraculously separate from other girls my age—but what felt so much worse was that I'd been dumb enough to buy it. Narcissism had led me to believe every word.

Craig probably noticed the torment play out on my face and said quickly, "I'm sorry. That's none of my business."

"No, it's fine. I'm going to go."

"I'm sorry, Ashley," he said and he just stood there with his handful of broken glass.

I went back into the apartment and gathered up my

things, humiliated that I'd been nebbish enough to bring a toothbrush like the neurotic kid I was. I walked to the parking lot, sat down in my car and began to cry. Eventually, I pulled myself together and drove home.

I didn't ever talk to Jesse again. I never even saw him again. I heard later that his financial situation got so bad that he could no longer afford coke and he switched to speed. Craig moved out and Jesse started doing so much speed that he couldn't pay utilities, so he did speed in the dark. I heard he moved to Tennessee or Texas or somewhere, a few months later, after he met a girl on the Internet.

I don't tell this story to air out just how bad my judgment was as a teenager. Almost everyone's judgment is pretty bad as a teenager, there's nothing really special about mine. Even the reasonably intelligent, cautious to the point of neurotic ones like myself are still presented with the opportunity to make terrible decisions (constantly). I almost made one such terrible decision.

But I didn't. What's disturbing is that I went through this brief, burning romantic affair with an older man—that thankfully nothing came of—and I didn't learn shit. The tricky thing about learning from your mistakes is you have to actually make those mistakes. With Jesse, I'd narrowly avoided them. The whole thing didn't equip me with a modicum of better judgment. The only thing that did happen is I became more reclusive for a few months and showed no interest in dating.

One happy thing that came out of this, though, is I realized I'm lucky to have had my parents, who trusted my judgment enough and subsequently did not restrict any access to

Jesse. If they had, I may have actually made that mistake because everything about him was already so appealing; letting
him symbolize total rebellion on top of that might have made
him irresistible. Most of the kids I knew in high school who
lost their virginity to assholes did so after sneaking out bedroom windows.

Granted, if your teenage daughter shows a romantic interest in the local coked-up unemployed actor with a taste for
young girls, you could take a more hands-on approach to par-
enting as opposed to just hoping for the best. The option is
there.

FEAR OF PROMISCUITY

The dumbest thing about the Jesse situation is how pointless it was. Sure it made me miserable, but when you're a shy, insecure, socially inept teenager, you're ripe to be exploited by anyone with a superego and a driver's license.

One day, at the junior college, I ran into the boy with black hair from my sociology class. He asked me out on a date, I said yes, we spent the evening playing pool at a pool hall and feeling very adult. Then we sat in his car before he took me home and I, true to my abject ineptitude, said, "What have we established here?" He said he didn't know and wisely waited a few more weeks to ask me out again.

We started seeing each other and he became my first "serious" boyfriend—by "serious" I mean as per some inscrutable equation of time together, mutual affection, and sexual activity—and was my first of practically every major formative sexual event. We had almost nothing in common except that we liked comic books and enough movies to feel bonded in the way teenagers find meaningful. He had a car and a grown-up job and his parents were nice to me. He was also a lot of fun and astoundingly good-looking.

He broke up with me after about six months because I was needy and mercurial and annoying. I picked fights and demanded unreasonable things. When I was that age—at this point, seventeen—I didn't think about how accumulating pointless arguments affected the health of my relationships. I just thought about getting what I wanted all the time. It took about a month of crying and gestures and proclamations to convince him to take me back.

There was a catch. He'd just moved into a new apartment with a bunch of dude roommates. They got a beer pong table and there were *Playboy* centerfolds over holes in the walls. He was at the age of being easily impressed with himself, that time of life when it's okay to display one's enormous DVD collection and not hide it away in a shameful place. Sometimes they cooked poppies that grew in neighboring yards, trying to make opium tea. It never worked, but the power of suggestion being what it is always made them behave like idiots when they drank it. What all of this meant was that he finally had a lot of freedom and he wanted to keep it that way. He was happy to keep seeing me but he didn't want to do so "exclusively."

I was desperate to have him back so I agreed. This was not a decision I was prepared to make and so began perhaps the darkest period of my adolescence, which was in no way particularly dark considering how every emotion is so razorous when you're seventeen. What I mean to say is that this was mine.

His obsession with sex became more ruthless. He told me in unwavering but never pornographic detail about other girls. He seemed most proud of the ones considered "dirtiest" by his peers: one nicknamed Typhoid Mary and another one who blew the dealer next door for coke. I'm lucky he was religious about protection with them and I was religious about protection with him, because I could have a lot more to regret these days if it weren't for that. I have to thank the California public school system's sex education, which taught me about herpes and syphilis and gonorrhea and did a phenomenal job of convincing my teenage self that unprotected sex outside the confines of committed, monogamous relationships was for insane people (it still is).

I've cultivated quite a lot of shame over this, because I didn't stick up for myself. I knew that the anguish in me was growing with each story I heard about some other girl and, to his credit, he was always very frank with me. I think he reasoned that if he remained direct and honest, the ball was always in my court. I had all the data I needed to make decisions for myself. The problem was I didn't have the spine.

This is a kind of classic bullshit move people play with one another. It takes a certain amount of adulthood to realize that being honest doesn't make you good, it just makes you honest. You can be completely open and direct about your flaws but it doesn't absolve you of them. Hopefully we can all agree that lying is awful, but it's important to add that being frank about your own awfulness doesn't make you less awful. It makes you easier to identify.

I'm not histrionic or vain enough to use words like "abuse" with respect to this situation; not only was I an effectively willing participant, I was also inoculated by his directness. Yet things began to accumulate that chipped away at my self-worth. Eventually, it felt like I would endure anything to remain unhappy. I was paralyzed: fearful of being away from him, vigilant with him near.

Maybe it was the bottle of lubricant he kept on the nightstand beside his bed, something never required for our purposes but an ever-present reminder of his activities with others. Maybe it was inviting me to a screening of a tape he made of two drunk girls fooling around in his bed. Maybe it was finding out that his roommates casually referred to me as Wednesday, owing to the day of the week that I was the girl in his room. Maybe it was when he admitted to me that he jerked off to the nightmarish anal rape scene in the movie *Irreversible*. A couple of times. Maybe it was when he told me that I was very innocent, which he "liked too," but part of the reason he wanted to be with other girls was my innocence made me unsuitable for the kind of violent sex he liked. This was fair enough as, having only been with him, sex was a mostly undiscovered frontier and doing anything that wasn't regular old missionary was practically a space mission. Still, it's never nice to hear that the reason for your bottomless torment is your own sexual inadequacy. By the time I came across a numbered list he kept of every girl he'd slept with in chronological order, I was so hollowed out that I scanned the list and saw my name—at thirteen, at seventeen, at nineteen and twenty-two with strangers names' in between and so on—and I felt nothing.

Part of my reason for telling this story, despite that it's still a dull pain in me, is to prove to myself that I don't have to feel shame over how someone else treated me and not to judge myself by coping with the heartache in a way I now recognize as weak. Part of it is to say that no one should feel ashamed of who they were at seventeen, unless they are the same. No one springs fully formed from their parents, able to identify goodness and decency and what we're willing to put up with in a partner; we have to learn. Part of it is to affirm that I don't mean to demonize him, because I don't think he was actually terrible to me so much as he was terribly suited to me; as far as sex-crazed teenage boys go, he wasn't remarkable in his appetite, but he was distinguished by his unwillingness to lie. Part of it is to record that honesty is not necessarily a virtue, let alone one meaningful enough to offset a corresponding set of vices.

I must also admit this period of my life instilled in me an unfair albeit permanent distrust of promiscuity. This time so soured me on the concept of casual sex that I sometimes still suppress a pang of judgment when I hear about messy hookups and one-night stands. It is a little Pavlovian negative association burnt into my heart and nothing more. In my right mind, I understand this is bigotry.

In a very important way, he didn't go about his promiscuity badly: he was frank, made no effort to conceal his activities, used protection meticulously and, as far as he was concerned, I was fully aware and fine with it. Because I said I was. I thought I could handle it, I tried, it hurt more and more and I became so sick with it all that it hardly stung any. I just took it.

But the most powerful lesson I learned in all of this? Don't date people you don't really like. They may pull off long hair and be charming and have lots of friends, but if you don't have anything to talk about and you don't respect each other, there's no point. There comes a time in many bad relationships when you realize that the other person is hilariously incongruous with you and your tastes and your values and, when you become an adult, the adult thing to do is listen to that realization because it will save you a lot of time.

With this first "serious" relationship, that moment came after months of enduring so much sadness. It was not the bottle of lubricant or the list of conquests with my name appearing again and again alongside the names of girls less virtuous on account of their anonymity. It was not his unapologetic want to fuck other girls with whom he could do things deemed too advanced or illicit for me. It was this: one day, I found a brand-new copy of the *Tao Te Ching* on his desk.

Thanks to my upbringing, I have an aggressive dislike of Westerners purporting to practice Eastern religion. I grew up beside many selfish, nasty, sanctimonious kids who came from money hailing themselves as Shintoists, for example, because they wanted to rebel against "the establishment" and they liked anime. Once I saw a woman at a Whole Foods sushi counter harangue a soft-spoken sushi chef for daring to use the same knife on separate (but both vegetarian) sushi rolls. He apologized profusely, but she insisted he make new rolls all over again and chastised him the entire time he did so, accusing him of thoughtlessness and not taking pride in his work. When he finished, having discarded the first rolls, she accepted the new batch, put them in her cart, prayered her hands at her chest and said curtly, "Namaste," before stomping off. This is, of course, no fault of the East's but it is exquisitely embarrassing for us in the West, having birthed and nurtured that rare beast, the "asshole Buddhist."

There I was in his room, under his towering stacks of action movie DVDs and beside his brand-new computer already made sluggish by an astonishing quantity of pornography. I picked up the book and saw its unbent spine and its pristine cover and said, "What's this?"—knowing full well what it was but smugly suspicious he didn't.

"Oh," he said, immediately trying to play it cool, "it's this really cool book that's, like, poetry but about how you should live your life." He paused and seemed to decide that he could do it more justice, then added, "It's about simpleness and it's just really cool. I'm really into it."

"Huh."

I drove home the next morning and he no doubt spent the following night fucking some girl I didn't know. Yet it was our exchange that plagued me and, for once, not the knowledge that I'd be sleeping alone while he was sleeping with someone else. I sat in bed that night thinking to myself that something about this smacked of behavior I actually couldn't abide.

Within a week or two, he had changed his profile across various social networks. Under religious views—which, if filled in, is never a good sign—went the curious phrase "Philosophical Taoism." My first thought was everything I knew to be true about this guy was diametrically opposed to what rudimentary knowledge I had of Taoism. It seemed, if nothing else, disingenuous to go waltzing into hundreds of years of nuanced reasoning and say, "This flatters my idea of myself. Now I shall gild my social media presence."

I knew in this exact moment that a vain, sex-crazed teenager whose only want was to play beer pong until he passed out inside of a stranger probably neither grasped nor sincerely cared for any text concerned with applying thoughtfulness to living. I probably didn't need to confirm with Laozi that this boy was unable to attune himself to the ineffable while having sex competitively. Or that it seemed impossible for him to revere the "mysterious female" while choking her with his cock.

My second thought was, *If I start using "philosophical" as an adjective, will it make everything I do sound more important?*

It was right then I got over it. I was so repulsed by this affront to critical thought that I managed to tear myself out. It wasn't all the humiliation and suffering that severed my deep, urgent emotional attachment. It was him becoming a Taoist on the Internet.

This cultural dilettantism was actually quite a beautiful expression of a fundamental difference of ours: I think that philosophy comes from introspection and consideration and discipline (which is why I have little will for it); he thought it came from spending six dollars at a mall bookstore, deciding it flattered him and then trotting off to the Internet to make sure changes in his relationship with the infinite were reflected online. Which is to say, I think philosophy is the activity of critical thought, he apparently thought philosophy was the absence of it. It was not everything else he did to me; it was old-fashioned, oblivious, self-serving hubris.

It's unfortunate I internalized his behavior and found it so objectionable that it formed my own bias. However, I can appreciate how he required of me an introspection and self-knowledge to eventually grow from that. He was the architect of a "Choose Your Own Sexual Hang-Up Adventure," in my heart. Although it took me eight years (or so) to get out of that midnight in an abandoned amusement park of my psyche, it was a valuable journey out and I won't begrudge him. Though I do hope, someday, he has a girl.

Besides, teenage heartbreak is devastating regardless of context. All feelings are at once more lucid and baroque when we're seventeen. If he didn't break my heart, someone else would have.

To those of you who think it's a bit hypocritical for me to praise my own coming to terms with an unfair bias while at the same time admitting I left a man out of what was ultimately an act of religious intolerance, I say, "Excellent work."

PARENTS

I think one of the greatest challenges to dating—at all ages—
is parents. Not your own, obviously, there's nothing you can
do about your own parents so they're not really a "challenge"
so much as a nuisance. I mean your significant other's parents.
Most of those I've encountered have just despised me.
Strangely, the ones who didn't despise me were the ones that
despised their sons, so there was probably a connection there.

I had a brief two-month faux relationship right around
age fifteen that didn't go far past the hand-holding stage. He
was crazy. He was clinically crazy. Once, his mother took my
hands and looked me really deep in the eyes and said, "Ashley,
you're just too good for him. Someday you'll realize that."
That was intense. It kind of made me wince at the time. Still,
I'm touched she brought it to my attention.

I had another boyfriend with a mother who openly loathed
me. She had a blunt, abrasive character in social situations and

was extremely childlike in her affect: denim smock dresses, braided pigtails affixed to her graying head with little plastic barrettes and giant Coke-bottle glasses, behind which she'd blink with animal bewilderment. Despite this—and her habit of clapping when the family dogs entered the room—she was exceptionally cruel and prone to hysterical fits of screaming rage when she disliked something. Basically, she was the quirky, adorable child from every juice commercial you've ever seen, only add forty years and ill will.

The moment I really understood this collision of simpleness and nastiness was right when I decided what college I wanted to attend, a college I happened to be very excited about. I ended up getting, for the sake of brevity, something like but not quite the equivalent of a classics degree. Which is funny, in this economy, because I really could have just taken $160,000 out of the bank—someone else's bank account, mind you, because I don't have that money—spent it all on acid and gotten to the bottom of things myself. At least I would have talked to some cool trees or something. But no, I graduated college in an abysmal recession with a degree in Reading Aristotle Good. And not even that good. Reading Aristotle Serviceably, that was my major.

The point is this is something I really wanted to do and I was so proud when I got in. In retrospect, I shouldn't have been because it wasn't remotely hard. It's not like they're turning kids away from the Reading Aristotle Serviceably program at the school no one's heard of in the middle of the New Mexican desert.

Regardless, I was over at this early boyfriend's house for dinner the day I decided I wanted to attend this college. His parents were visibly relieved to learn there was an end to our relationship in sight. They asked me what I was going to study there and I said, "Classics."

My then-boyfriend's mother looked up from her kids' menu food—because the rest of the family ate like adults but she ate butter noodles and chicken fingers for dinner every night—and she just said, "What . . . a waste . . . of time."

I was so startled by the sheer force of her judgment that I had no idea what to say.

She continued: "Why would anyone do that?"

"Uh. I just think that . . . well, it'd be great to read books, I think that would make me a better writer. And I'd like to read classics so I can learn about the history of the Western world," and I stuttered something about seeing its "progression of thought." Which isn't terrible, really, because it's not like one day some politician or television producer or ad man decided that man has a soul or that a system of morality should exist or that the planets move in a certain way or that parallel lines don't intersect (or, eventually, that they do). Those things had to come from some place and no one's a monster for being curious about where. It is monstrous, though, to ridicule teenagers who care about their education, while the absolute most monstrous thing is to lack the courage to speak up for oneself in moments of minor conflict and then, having stewed for years, write a vicious takedown of everyone who ever wronged you, especially that woman who wore rainbow striped socks with the toes in them. Well, fuck her.

After I'd given my little apology for studying classics, she replied in the same tone of barely bridled disgust, "I don't think any of that stuff matters."

I'm still baffled that an adult would say this to a teenager. I don't think you should disparage the dreams of terminally insecure, ultimately well-meaning teenagers who always offer to be the designated driver. Unless, obviously, their dreams are stupid. Like wanting to break the world record for having the most billiard balls in your mouth or major in communications.

I kind of nodded, as if to say, "I totally get that," because I was a coward who thought placating people and being blindly respectful was going to get me somewhere in life. "Yeah, I mean, it's not like becoming a lawyer or something." Which, by the way, my mother still wants, though the only reasoning she's ever put forth is I'll acquire lots and lots of skirt suits. Something opaque about skirt suits.

My then-boyfriend's mother frowned deeply and looked up, above me, now appearing to think aloud more than challenge me directly. "I just don't understand why anyone would want to read a bunch of books by dead white men."

I looked at her and her long, messy, grade-school braided pigtails and I regarded the funny cat-shaped brooch she always wore on her breast like a billboard of suspended adolescence and all I could think was, *Funny, I don't know why anyone would want to sit around in this darkened house all day crafting with macaroni noodles in between shitting out unremarkable children. But I'll tell you what I do understand: why your son fucking hates women.* But you can't say that to someone with a plateful of chicken fingers and butter noodles. It's selfish to ruin things like that.

Miraculously, this mother was not the greatest source of grief from a significant other's parent I've encountered.

Not even close. Next in line was the mother of a guy I dated when I was a few years older. This guy was also a bit of a woman-hating prick, but his parents were much more erudite. His mother was outwardly a very nice person but also passive-aggressive and undermining. Her favorite game—if I were to give it a name—was Telling Stories About All the Girls My Son Has Known Who Are Better Than You. Although I didn't take her seriously enough to be hurt by this, it was still exhausting to live on the receiving end of her thick-headed affectation of urbanity and withering disdain.

For example, I'd be siting in this woman's living room. I'd like to tell you I was reading Plato or Chaucer or Shakespeare or something that reflects well on me but I was almost certainly doing a puzzle intended for small children, wearing a jean jacket, and watching Animal Planet. So whatever infantile thing I was doing in the living room was unimportant, but she would come walking through with a basket of laundry and she would see me sitting there with the puzzle and then she'd stop and look off with a far-and-away expression, misty almost, and say, "Oh, that's so strange."

I'd look up.

"I just got déjà vu. You reminded me of someone."

"Oh? Who?" And I walked into the trap with huge, innocent eyes because she was instigating conversation. Maybe she liked me!

"I was just thinking of his first girlfriend, Colleen."

"Oh." And I looked down because that's a bizarre thing to say.

Of course she elaborated. "She really broke his heart. He was so cut up over that, he just stayed in his room for weeks.

He was devastated, I didn't think he would ever recover. I mean," and here she would pause thoughtfully and tilt her head to one side as if to give her statement heft through more adroit consideration, "she had to go to Yale and do what was best for her. I think that's why he took it so hard, because they didn't break up over something bad happening or their feelings for each other going away. They broke up only because she had to pursue her dreams of studying architecture in the Ivy League."

Side note: the college I attended—where I met her son, incidentally—accepts approximately everyone who applies, though it is renowned for its astonishing rate of attrition (about half of the freshmen class makes it to graduation, a statistic that would horrify more arid institutions). I've never been one to be impressed by the name of a college, and I think higher education is what you make of it, and you get out what you put in, and also, the undergraduate experience of the Ivy League in particular holds little glamour as far as I'm concerned thanks to its legacy of grade inflation and dynastic admissions policies. I also recognize that these thoughts are extremely convenient for someone who attended a college roughly all people can get into. The brochures explain it away by suggesting most students self-select (and there is truth to that), but that is a kind of honey-laced wormwood we drink while discussing Lucretius with other eighteen-year-old assholes who smoked too much weed to get into Brown.

Regardless. She wasn't done: "Colleen was brilliant. I mean, obviously. And so beautiful . . . and so accomplished. His father and I always knew that she was going to do something very special. She was going to leave her mark, you know? There are so few people like that, where you meet them and you just know they're going to change the world. Colleen was like that. Just an extraordinary girl," and she shifted the weight of the laundry hamper to one side and shrugged, affecting enormous compassion as she looked down at me, hard at work on a puzzle of puppies spilling out of a basket, and she'd say, "but he seems really happy with you."

Before you become practically impressed by her contempt, I want to drive home the point that this was an extremely typical example of Telling Stories About All the Girls My Son Has Known Who Are Better Than You. She even had a favorite variation on the game, which she played whenever she tired of other narratives. It was called Laura—with Whom He Went to High School—Is a Model and you can probably guess how it's played, but it went like this: she was obsessed with reminding me that Laura, with whom he went to high school, was a model. If you think it's hard to tease more than one conversation out of a seemingly very simple, discrete piece of data, you are dead wrong. No visit, whether for a weekend trip or weeks in close quarters, was complete without a reminder of Laura from High School.

My then-boyfriend's mother and her great venomous showpiece always began with a wistful look far away from me and then went like this: "I saw his old friend Laura today at the grocery store. All the boys were just in love with Laura. She was so tall," and then she'd look at me because I'm five-eleven and say, "a little taller than you. She must have been almost six feet tall. And, God, she was so thin, so thin," and then she'd look at me, up and down, say nothing, and continue. "She had the most beautiful skin and long beautiful brown hair. Just the most gorgeous girl. The kind of girl that you only see once in a lifetime. So, of course, she had to go and become a model. I think as soon as she graduated high school, she went off to Europe to walk the designer runways. I knew she was going to be a model, from the time she was thirteen. I remember seeing her when I was chaperoning a dance once and she just lit up the room," and she'd pause again, because pauses were how she indicated the encroach of the killing blow, and she'd say, "She had such a crush on my son."

Her sheer commitment to the game and its brutal passive aggression was at least amusing. I acclimated quickly and learned not to take it personally because it seemed every time Laura from High School was in play conversationally, her presence would expand upward and become taller and thinner and somehow, impossibly, more beautiful. Every time. The game and its increasingly obvious exaggerations brought me much bittersweet entertainment until the night I actually met Laura from High School.

I was in his hometown for Christmas, and all the kids who had moved away were back, catching up over drinks and pool games in the local dive bar. Right around ten o'clock, a young woman walked in and parted the crowd and many eyes were on her. It was Laura from High School, I knew instantly, and I can confirm she was indeed taller than me. That, though, was the only shred of truth.

I'm not going to disparage Laura from High School (too much) because my dislike of her was colored almost entirely by my then-boyfriend's mother. Almost. It was not her fault that my then-boyfriend's mother had weaved for her this kind of outlandish folktale that didn't line up with anything real.

Laura from High School was absolutely not a model and that's no disrespect to her. She was pretty in a robustly conventional way. She had the kind of forgettable, blandly attractive features that would make for a mean toothpaste commercial. But this isn't about feelings of vindication regarding Laura from High School; this is about my then-boyfriend's mom being a liar.

One thing did really strike me about Laura from High School—and you could tell just by looking at her. A few years ago, she had indeed been very desirable and presumably very popular, but that was the apex of her existence. Life for Laura from High School was never going to approach the exhilarating, impossible high of being hot shit at seventeen—she would never be Laura from Anthropology Class or Laura from the Office.

Have you ever met someone who said high school or college years are the best of your life? As soon as anyone ever says that, you should just X them permanently. They're done; they don't have anything to offer you; they are husks of humanity shuffling blind through an eternal dark. Worse still, they will drag you down with them in a flurry of insisting the jeans they're currently wearing were purchased at sixteen. Anyone who has ever made a positive impact on society does not think of high school as the gold standard of human happiness.

Within moments of entering the bar, fratty satellites moved into orbit around her, guys in visors who still hadn't let go. She talked to them without seeming to pay attention, glancing over their heads and checking the bar for more important characters, clearly relishing not needing to uphold her end of conversation. After a while, she split off into a hallway, where the bathrooms were located. I saw my opportunity. Not in, like, an assault way, obviously.

I was pretty fascinated to learn as much as I could about her and observe her in a secluded habitat. I ran into the hallway and took my place in line. There I stood behind the fabled Laura from High School, staring pretty unsubtly. She noticed, because she was a small-town pretty girl, which meant she always expected people to stare at her. We accidentally made eye contact a few times and on the third or fourth, we both held it long enough to require some next step.

"Hi!" I said.

She arched her nose and hesitated so I'd recognize that I was out of line by speaking to her. She said reluctantly, "Hi."

I kept staring now, because I was even more curious about her than before.

Laura from High School looked away. She'd glance back and again look away in a huff. With each cycle, she became more irritated until finally she said, "Do I know you?"

"No," I said, in my most sprightly, aw-shucks homeschooler diction.

". . . Okay," she said.

I tried to stop staring at her, but by this point, our interplay of glances and looks away had become enthralling. She seemed urgent for the thrill of scowling at me and then looking away.

"I'm Ashley," I said, putting out my hand.

She looked at my hand for a moment. She did not put out hers. Instead, she mustered all the judgment contained within her and said, "Are you, like, a lesbian or something?"

"Totally!" I replied and then, as if to lay her down gently, added, "But you're not my type."

Her time came and she entered the restroom. I wandered off. The last thing I'll note about Laura from High School is that, later, I waved to her enthusiastically as I was leaving and heard her describe me to one of her fratty acolytes as "the dyke that tried to follow [her] into the bathroom."

Meeting Laura from High School proved that I was never going to be a good enough son's girlfriend to my then-boyfriend's mother. I tried, though: I even went to his little sister's dance recital. If you've never been to a middle school-er's dance recital, I would describe it as "the most anguish a human can endure without suffering physical pain." It is three hours with one sickly sweet fifteen-minute break of eleven-year-old girls in unitards doing cautiously incompetent inter-pretive dance to currently chart-topping popular music. If you become a parent, you must remember to never ask someone not a blood relative of the child onstage to attend one of these hallucinatory nightmares. It is the single worst thing you can imagine that doesn't involve harm to you or your loved ones.

Until you date a Mormon, which really distorts your under-standing of being dealt a poor hand.

For the moment, all you need to know about him is that he wasn't very religious but his father, mother and extended family sure were. This was fine because, though I like to make fun of it sometimes, I'm not intolerant at all of religion or people of faith. Some of the smartest people in history have believed in God, people vastly smarter and more talented than myself and almost certainly you who are reading this, unless your name is Homer, Dante Alighieri, John Milton, Fyodor Dostoevsky or Isaac Newton. You can't say that people who believe in God and practice religion are all idiots. But the Mormon's parents made it really hard.

Once, I was staying with his family for Christmas Eve and, that morning, they invited us to church. Which is to say, they forced me to go to church with them by stating there would be no other option. That if I wanted to stay in their house, I would be accompanying them to church that morning. On a practical level, how am I supposed to wake up at seven a.m. and tolerate a God I don't believe in? It's not like they made coffee.

The Mormon himself had a kind of agitated resignation when it came to his parents and he wasn't going to speak up on my behalf. Because I was all of twenty years old, unable to afford a last-minute hotel room and in the middle of Colorado without any place to go as an alternative, I did what I thought was my only option: go to church with them and cry the whole time. Not gasping, snot-filled sobs or anything that would make a scene—I have way too much pride for that sort of thing—more like a quiet, defeated-but-dignified weeping. Like a Confederate soldier. There I sat in that church on Christmas Eve, completely astonished that I'd been made to worship, convincing myself I was a Faulkner character and this was a picture of reticent Southern dignity in the face of overwhelming loss.

Some people might say, "Oh, shut up, Ashley, they just wanted you to come with them to church for like two hours for one morning in your life. They were putting you up!" But no, actually, what they were doing was shanghaiing someone to church. If the tables were turned, no one would defend me if I demanded they spend Christmas Eve getting shitfaced on bourbon and having guilt-free sex with someone they weren't married to. That they'd have no choice if they were staying at my house. I wouldn't do this because I'm not a bigot. It was the most I've ever hated religion in my entire life, the morning I sat in a Mormon church refusing to eat the sacrament of cubed Wonder Bread they passed around and miming hymns through bitter tears.

I must admit the Mormon's parents had a longstanding dislike of me going much further back than this fateful Christmas Eve morning. It actually all began within the first hour of our introduction. The Mormon and I had been dating for a few months at this point and it was time to finally meet his parents, so we drove about seven hours to Colorado for Thanksgiving. We showed up and they were distant but not cold, excited to see their son but understandably less excited to see the physical manifestation of his soul's eternal damnation. Because—and this is a very shitty thing about being a girl—people think they know your sexual proclivities just by how you talk or dress or generally conduct yourself. Even though I'd packed every knee-grazing skirt I owned for the trip and weeded out any necklines that dipped below my scandalous collarbone, I wasn't fooling them.

Tangentially, I don't know what it is about me that makes people so certain I'm "very" sexually experienced, as if that's a sort of thing you can tell by looking at someone. I've been told variously that people think I'm promiscuous because I "speak my mind," because I "wear short dresses," because I'm "assertive," because I "wear lots of eye makeup," because I wear "heels "and "low-slung pants," because I "drink whiskey."

So it sounds like all of these assumptions are pretty arbitrary and, fundamentally, sexist. Personally, I think the real reason people assume I'm sexually active is my wide stance. It always looks like I'm recovering from something.

The Mormon's parents took one look at me and determined immediately that I was not saving it for marriage, much less marriage in a Mormon temple (even though they give you your own planet, which sounds great). They had met me moments before and shook my hand and somehow they just knew their son and I had pulled over to have sex at least twice on the drive there. Maybe the second time we didn't even pull over, because why would you make a seven-hour drive longer if you don't have to? And they were right. *They were absolutely right.*

But! I actually intercepted their suspicion early on and almost started turning things around. His mother and I had both studied art history so we ended up having a polite conversation about Hellenistic sculpture. She seemed cautiously impressed. Better still, it was extremely easy to find common ground with his father, because I'm a great cook and he's a misogynist. Before I knew it, I was getting on surprisingly well with my Mormon boyfriend's parents.

At one point, his father became so enthused by my interest in cooking that he began describing a recipe for pasta sauce that he loved despite its sounding totally gross. It amounted to buying store-bought sauce, putting it in a pan and adding hamburger meat. Which isn't really a recipe when you think about it. More like just combining things. I don't buy two paintings and put them beside each other and then claim to have created a newer, better painting. That's crazy. But I wanted him to like me (an instinct that results in approximately ninety-nine percent of my grief as a human) and I didn't yet know these were the kinds of people who, a year later, were going to drag me to church despite me being a separate individual from them.

He finished telling me the recipe and, up to that point, our conversation had mostly been about my personal interest in cooking and not much as it related to his son. He then motioned to his son, my boyfriend, my first adult boyfriend, my college boyfriend and said, "Do you cook much for him?"

And, because I am a hopeless idiot, I replied, "I cook him breakfast!"

He flinched. He visibly flinched.

What is completely devastating about this situation is my answer was actually a very earnest, nonsexual one. What I meant to say is that we both lived on campus and didn't have all that much access to a cooking facility, with the exception of morning meals during which the dining hall staff would set up a make-your-own-omelet station. You'd stand in line for a few minutes (judging others on the quality and execution of their omelets) and then take your place at this podium in front of a little hot plate and pan. Spread out before you were chopped vegetables and shredded cheese so you could customize your own omelet. It was the only actual cooking I could do, living on campus. So, when I told his father I "cooked him breakfast," I meant that I would make him omelets in the dining hall before class in the morning and it was really the only kitchen time afforded to me. Granted, we were absolutely having sex the night before, but there was still a really wholesome aspect to my response.

Let me tell you something about dealing with your significant other's parents: don't remind them you're fucking their kid inside the first hour of meeting them. Especially if they're religious. Especially if they're Mormon. Let that go unsaid. They find the whole concept unsettling enough without you just letting the cat of the bag.

I'll tell you something else: there is absolutely no bouncing back from this. I tried, I really tried, I babbled something incoherent to the effect of, "Because they have a make-your-own-omelet station in the dining hall!" And then I tried to really sanitize it and said, "We meet there! He comes down from his dorm and I come from my dorm—we come from our respective dorms!—where we sleep, after studying, and we meet before class. Before class. In the morning. Our dorms are really far away." But his father's look of equal parts horror and recognition didn't dissipate and in fact, over the next two years that I dated the Mormon, kind of seemed to harden there.

Even though it was the most awful and uncomfortable moment I have ever shared with a boyfriend's parents, the thing about it that still haunts me is my naïveté: I really was speaking to being devoted and adoring. I just wanted to make him omelets. In the morning, before class, at the expense of last-minute studying. And you know what? Most parents would think that makes me a great girlfriend.

STRIPPERS

I don't talk to a lot of sex workers but that's probably because they can smell fear. Still, from what I've deduced, there are three prevailing opinions in popular culture about what kind of person becomes a sex worker. First off, let's just define our terms: by sex worker, I mean adult film stars, prostitutes and strippers. Strippers may not be explicitly paid for sex, but they certainly trade in it, so I'm counting them even though this flippant characterization may be a bit controversial. There are various schools of thought on whether or not strippers are indeed sex workers and I'm sure these various schools align themselves with progressivism in a way that I should do some rote Googling to discern. I chose not to because as soon as the Internet becomes a barometer of morality, we should probably all just die.

The three predominant views about why women become sex workers are as follows:

Whether for reasons of misogyny or guilt or moralizing, camp 1 suspects that the sex worker found his or her way into the industry through unsavory means like abuse, molestation, bullying, self-loathing, addiction, desperation, poverty or a pathological and relentless desire to be filled with dicks. These people buy into the stereotype of the damaged whore. They are bad or misinformed people who believe women in short dresses were all molested as children. They also tend to be the kinds of people who correct your grammar, which is even more repulsive.

The next camp is responsible for what I like to call the narrative of the jocose young porn star. Camp 2 is firmly a part of the sex industry and claims that it all began because they wanted to get laid so they picked themselves up, zipped closed their suitcases and moved to Southern California with their mouths open. Simultaneously, plucky Iowa-corn-fed hookers around New York are always giving anonymous interviews about the lavish lifestyles they lead, pulling in ten grand for a weekend of private jets and high fashion and—well, I don't know what rich people do. Put steak on lobster? Maybe inside of lobster? In other words, the more outspoken sex workers (or at least the ones with journalist friends) boast of the thrilling and well-compensated lifestyle of someone professionally good at sex. These people likely also suspect they are tolerable on cocaine. They are wrong.

As for the third camp, they're similar in kind to camp 2 but there's an important distinction: camp 3 is pervaded by an impenetrable cloud of pseudo-intellectualism. For them, it's not about steak and lobster parfait; it's about a yearning, a quest for some elusive abstraction. Camp 3 are those millionth-generation feminists who graduate from a small liberal arts school, move to New York to be writers or interns at literary magazines or *muses*, but wind up prostitutes because apparently the more you know about continental philosophy, the more you can charge. These are almost exclusively English majors and art history enthusiasts who get their toes wet on sugar daddy social networking sites and then transition into full-time hooking which then transitions into the keeping of anonymous blogs about decadent masked parties in the dead of night in Venice and cavernous exposed-brick Lower East Side apartments with thirty-foot ceilings filled with books about the Hapsburg Empire and expensive wine while disaffected lounge covers of Joy Division spin on vintage turntables forever. The only difference between anonymous pseudo-intellectual prostitute bloggers and smug assholes who never had an original thought are student loans. Ultimately, what really separates these individuals from camp 2 is they've convinced themselves they're actually doing this for progressivism.

Of the three main theories of who goes into sex work and what they do while there—whether it's that all sex work stems from abuse or that all sex work is like a huge orgasm party with no STDs ever or the same thing I just said only more *cerebral*—none of them are particularly compelling. I don't think all sex workers are victims of abuse, I don't believe all porn stars love their jobs or the industry and I absolutely don't buy that anonymous sex writers on the Internet are injecting glamour into women's rights by sucking dick for money and blogging about it. Of course, there are plenty of reasonable, well-adjusted people who become sex workers. Unfortunately, reasonable people will never be the majority anywhere—or at least won't hire good publicists.

I have known a few sex workers. One was a smart, capable writer, quite talented and completely ordinary in her neuroses. Too ordinary, in fact, to elaborate on here. Another was a pseudo-intellectual call girl obsessed with herself and her modicum of (already incredibly niche) notoriety. The last was an ancient, wheezing pole dancer in the darkest, dankest strip club in Denver.

The pseudo-intellectual was a bony, ghoulish prostitute who talked exclusively about sex and her own accomplishments. I met her through a mutual friend at a bar. She took herself so gravely serious that I was shown naked pictures of her and prompted to write down the address of her blog within fifteen minutes of meeting her. Regarding those naked photos, I guess her photographer friend saw some merit in harshly lit portraits of topless women drooling fluid but I don't really go to bars for that. I go to bars for drinking. Smoking outside. Sometimes Erotic Photo Hunt. She did seem sincerely proud to have participated in the creation of art, which I guess suggests a level of sophistication the average fluid drooler lacks, so maybe that was ginkgo or ginseng or something running down her chest.

The stripper is the heart of our story. I found myself brought to a staggering conclusion about humanity beneath her podium one Friday night with three friends. At this point I was attending college in New Mexico and we had driven to Denver for a concert. The show got canceled but we went anyway because my life had no real substance and it was nice to just do things in different places.

I had originally planned the trip around two shows, one on a Friday night and one on a Saturday night (to justify the six-hour drive) and we figured we'd stay out all night in between or sleep in a cheap hotel room. We found out Friday morning that the first night's show was canceled because the singer of the headlining band was having throat (cocaine) problems. The driver of this road trip had consequently wanted to stay behind until Saturday because he'd ordered a fancy cattle guard off eBay and was enthused to ornament his Land Rover. I insisted we go a night early.

I was insistent, sadly, because I was suffering under terrible heartbreak, having just been dumped by my boyfriend of a year, the aforementioned Mormon (though we'd eventually get back together). He'd broken up with me a week before school started despite our plans to live together. He had decided instead to live in a Volkswagen van parked just off campus, which is a pretty gutting punchline about my appeal. Within four days of our breakup, I spotted him emerging from the dorm room of a shockingly pert freshman. I was devastated: she had the body of a *Sports Illustrated* swimsuit model and the face of a Sephardic Julia Roberts. Thanks to her predilection for cutoffs and bikini tops, I wanted to flee and get into some mild trouble in another state. I was persuasive enough that my friends and I pulled into Denver around ten thirty that Friday.

We didn't know anyone, we didn't know anywhere to go and it was before the ubiquity of smart phones, so we had no idea where we were or what was around us. Luckily, the driver was a bit of an enterprising social butterfly and pulled over to the first bar belching college kids onto the street. He promptly made some friends and learned that it was pledge week so all the frats were dry. He then got us directions to a house party. We showed up and no one recognized us so they assumed we were seniors and led us to the keg. Sometime later, we realized we were at the wrong party.

We eventually made it to the actual party and I ended up being the only girl in a group of about sixty frat boys. I was sitting alone, smoking sullenly, not drinking, thinking about the Mormon and trying to figure out what made me so insufferable* that he'd rather live in a Volkswagen van than live with me. I happened to be smoking an imported German cigarette (*unrelated) that one of my road trip companions had given me. A frat boy came up and asked what I was smoking and I answered, "Botschafters," and he said, "Pretty exotic. But not as exotic as these," and then with a stunning lack of irony, placed a tin of raspberry-flavored Camels on the table. He proceeded to tell me about his father's leatherworking business, which I guess explained the origin of his fringed suede vest and also made him overqualified for even the most brutal, harrowing, malevolent hatefuck in history.

After we had taken our fill of sixty white frat boys doing keg stands, chanting "Skeet skeet skeet" while others watched Dave Chappelle in the living room and laughed at what they perceived to be hilarious jokes about the fecklessness of black people, I demanded we go to a strip club. I'm not entirely sure why I suggested the strip club but I was nineteen and thought it would be a fun distraction and frankly, when you're nineteen, sometimes you want to be the girl who suggests going to a strip club because it makes you seem cool and unthreatened and therefore desirable. People can be pretty stupid this way.

After driving for a long, long time, we came upon a few places that looked like strip clubs from the outside but were twenty-one-and-over clubs. We pulled over and asked for directions a couple times but no one could direct us to anything specifically eighteen and over. We ended up procuring a phone book and calling around while driving aimlessly because college kids are actually deeply uncreative when it comes to behaving badly. They mostly just drink and fuck and discover things like Bret Easton Ellis and psilocybin, which they grow out of if they're decent in any meaningful capacity.

We got to the place around one in the morning. It was the only storefront in a near-abandoned strip mall. I don't remember much else about our surroundings because it was dark. We found the place, actually, not because it was marked in any eye-catching way (STRIPPERS. WATCH THEM.) but because there was a man in a really big shirt cooking hot dogs on a grill hitched to the back of his truck and selling them for a dollar. The billowing smoke led us to the entrance of the club.

When we walked in, we all felt that illicit thrill one experiences upon entering one's first strip club, falling into the low green lights amid KISS songs and disco ball revolutions. After we paid and got a ticket for one nonalcoholic beverage of our choosing, the first thing I saw was a breathtakingly beautiful young stripper on a podium. She looked like Aaliyah, with the same enigmatic almond-shaped eyes and straight dark hair concealing half her face. She was wearing a white catsuit unzipped and hanging around her hips. Her breasts were distractingly, memorably perfect, shaped and weighted so divinely that it took me a few moments to notice she was sobbing. She leaned over and began scraping up dollar bills as two men with cigars jeered at her like comic book villains. It was at this point I had a sickening feeling. I wondered if I wanted the next two hours of my life to take place there.

My friends went off to find a podium with empty seats and I went to the bathroom which, incidentally, featured mirrored floors. Because of the angle and situation of the stalls, you could pretty easily see into the vagina next to you. Fortunately, no one was using the toilets for their intended purposes, as both mirrors on either side of my stall revealed the grim reflections of labia on towering Lucite heels, groups of strippers leaning precariously over each other to snort lines off toilet tanks. I stood in the stall for a long time trying to stave off panic because I was thinking about the Mormon and how he'd probably be disgusted with me if he knew I was in such a shithole. I was also confused that these strippers weren't the cartoonish visions of sexuality with which I was familiar from television or the plucky fallen angels I knew from movies. Rather, they were what would happen if you stuck a pin in those and deflated them. Kind of dissolving and fundamentally tired. I had to get out of the bathroom.

I found my friends holding court at the podium of an ancient stripper with bleach-choked hair and an oppressed look. My three male friends were all sitting in a row and I took a place at the end, beside the driver. This is when I witnessed the stripper's shtick: she'd crouch down, facing the patron. She'd then lay his hands on the platform, palms up, placing each breast in each respective palm while she looked at him seductively. She smelled like an ashtray fire put out with an entire bottle of Crystal Palace and said her name was Amber. I'm pretty sure it was the first time any of them had ever touched fake breasts. I was curious too because they looked so heavy and the skin seemed stringy around them. I'm also pretty sure her name wasn't actually Amber. That's another thing I learned from her: strippers have a utilitarian attitude when it comes to truth.

I watched her go through the line of my friends. The first two were baby faced and innocent and looked unsettled by the whole thing. When she got to the driver—the ostensible leader, he was more charismatic and less compassionate than the others—she laid his hands on the table and leaned into them, her unnervingly blank gaze locked on his . . . then, with her veiny, humongous breasts in his hands, she abruptly glanced sideways at me and said to him, "This your girlfriend?"

The driver arched his lip in disgust (he was an asshole) (but: fair) and said, "No. She's . . . not really . . ." and, like it agonized him to have to explain, *"my type."*

The old stripper studied him for a long silent moment and then she tilted her head and looked to her right, like she was consulting the depths of that side of her brain. She got lost thinking and stared upward at the dark ceiling with a dense but contemplative look, overwhelmed by the vastness of the universe and humbled for it.

After a little longer she finally spoke, still with this leaden ponderous look, and said, "But . . . is there really such a thing as a type?" and then all four of us just sat back bathed in the swirling disco ball glow and "You Shook Me All Night Long" stopped playing and the dollar bills hovered in the air all around as we thought to ourselves, *Holy shit, is there? Is attraction arbitrary? Are "types" and "ideals" just social constructs?* But before we could beg her to expand, she just added in this piercing coke whine, "Where the fuck is Crystal? I've been up here for four fucking songs."

To make a long story shorter, we then spent a silent, surreal evening in a thirty-dollar-per-night hotel in a bad part of town and the show on Saturday was all right. We drove home after, all pretty sick of each other by the end of the weekend and not speaking. I remember being half asleep in the backseat of the car and thinking about the Mormon. Since the breakup, I'd been feeling so isolated and terrified no one would ever love me again, which at that moment I realized was just defeatist. You don't date by type and love is as much a learned trait as it is something that exists instantaneously. Most important, someone will always want you. That's what truck stops and shot bars are for. The stripper, Amber, had somehow managed to dislodge my fear of dying unloved and alone.

I sat in the backseat of the Land Rover and all I could think was there probably wasn't one person for everyone and all it took for me to realize such a thing was one person wondering it aloud with some honesty. I slipped into sleep and for the first time since the breakup, felt some contentment. Soon after, we crossed through Colorado into New Mexico where there exists an enormous, sprawling migration corridor and we smashed into an elk. We were all fine, but the impact did tremendous damage to the Land Rover's front end, damage that the cattle guard (sitting on the driver's doorstep) would have prevented.

To this day, I really cherish that moment between me and Amber. The opportunity to interact with her was a strange one that I'll always appreciate and that someone so different but just as dull or just as perceptive as anyone could offer real insight. I look back on the whole weird, crushing, distressing affair and think to myself that I was childish to be so afraid—and also that it was lame of Crystal to be such a bitch and leave Amber hanging like that.

SEX AND GOD

I don't recommend having sex with Mormons. I should qualify that, though, because I have pretty glowing things to say about the physical relationship I had with one. In fact, the sex itself was almost uniformly fantastic. I'm not really sure why that is, but I'm guessing it's because they're so outdoorsy and athletic, from all the milking cows or panning for gold. Though I don't actually know a lot about Mormons, what I do know is sex with the one I dated was great but all the other aspects that came along with it presented a problem. Mormons have a lot of guilt. And they get wasted after like three drinks.

As I've mentioned, I dated a Mormon guy for a few years and it didn't work out. Nowadays when people ask me why it fell apart, I usually shrug in a really hammy way and answer, "You can take the boy out of Salt Lake City, but you can't take the Salt Lake City out of the boy," mostly because I love canned statements and am intellectually dishonest. It's also stupid because he wasn't from Utah and most times people will just look at me in confusion and say, "Is that where he's from originally?" and I say, "No," and look away until they change the subject. What happened between the two of us was a lot more complicated than just a location or abstract concept being inside of someone. Tangentially, the decision to home-school is a serious one and you should make certain that it's the best thing for your child.

Here's the thing: I do have a soft spot for religion and courtesy and nice paintings of saints looking bummed and compassion and presents on Christmas and all that. There's something really lovely about religious ceremony; heretical assholes like myself don't have any elaborate initiations or big parties where we get lots of money, so I guess I want someone who'd insist on giving that experience to our offspring. Not believing in God or karma or a higher power or prevailing goodness is great because you can basically behave however you want, but on the flip side, your rites of passage aren't imbued with religious dignity and are instead a few grim bill-boards along the road that is increasing distance from youth as you hurtle toward solitary death.

For example, at sixteen, nonbelievers get a license. At eighteen, we're given the opportunity to enter a convenience store thinking we're going to purchase a pornographic maga-zine, until we find out it costs like ten fucking dollars and fuck that noise because it's all over the Internet for free. Turning twenty-one is obviously no big deal because you've already been shitfaced most good days of your life since turning four-teen and it's not like they start letting you drink *and* drive.

Then there's renting a car or getting a 401(k) or spending most nights suppressed under the frigid certainty that maybe you shouldn't have spent so much time hating your twenties (and imagining wrinkles) because it turns out that's the highlight of adulthood and it's a free fall from there.

In response, I seek out guys who have complicated relationships to whatever the almighty means to them. More plainly, if I had to sum up "my type," it would be a man with Christian values who doesn't believe in God. And brown hair. This has only worked out badly.

Luckily, the Mormon and I weren't meant to be together and broke up after a year. It was a perfectly acceptable college relationship with a mostly clean break and I figured things out in Denver and that would have all been great if we didn't get back together after a month. As I have mentioned, he spent the interim with this freshman who had an astonishing body. When we got back together, he was pretty overcome with guilt at having gone astray or already tired of using condoms, so he asked if I would accompany him to Mormon church so he could speak with the bishop. For guidance.

I should reiterate that the Mormon wasn't really Mormon and most of my jokes about it have been misleading. He was raised one but he started to question the church as a teenager, right about the time he started having sex (I've always suspected the two were related). By all outward appearances, he was thoughtful and logical and didn't really believe in God. Every now and again, though, I'd wonder if he had some repressed Mormon leanings, like when he shut off and became comatose with anguish after sex. I guess it never bothered me because I found him so refreshingly unencumbered by gender stereotypes.

I was receptive to this meet-the-bishop request primarily because I was relieved to be back together with him. I also found his old stubborn solace in spiritual guidance kind of romantic. I posited he wanted to see the bishop because bishops were stalwart authority figures from childhood, like Santa or Ronald Reagan or that guy who'd stand beyond the playground's chain-link fence for hours at a time, just silently regarding us as we played. Like an angel.

The church itself was this menacing, low, brutalist building that rose from a sprawling concrete parking lot flat atop the desert, which is weird because most Mormon temples look like the seventeenth hole of a miniature golf course. We'd made an appointment with the bishop but had to wait anyway, because I guess you can't shuck spiritual guidance out in thirty-minute increments, which makes sense because it's not like these guys have degrees in psychology or medicine or something real.

The interiors of Mormon churches are also incredibly weird because apparently Mormons believe Jesus was like Pocahontas. I looked at a ton of velvet paintings of Jesus breaking maize with little Aztec children and this is what I could deduce. The most distracting thing about these paintings is that Mormons also believe both Jesus and little groups of Aztec children all look like Hitler Youth. Or maybe they only had white paint? Also, I bet velvet paint is expensive because it's quite shiny, so it makes sense economically if the Central American natives and Middle Eastern Jews are the same color as the white people who attend this church. After all, running a church isn't anything like running a business and sometimes you have to cut corners.

We waited a long time on the bleachers of the church's vast, silent indoor basketball court and my boyfriend sat there, becoming increasingly nervous. He was spinning a basketball compulsively between his fingers, just staring ahead and saying nothing. I didn't know what he expected to get out of this, but whatever it was meant a lot. Every now and again a preteen girl in a bonnet would scuttle in and back out without making eye contact, probably to go work on some lemon squares for a bake sale.

I too grew increasingly nervous, though not for the same reasons. I had been in only a handful of churches before. I'm pretty principled in my agnosticism, so I always swore I would never enter a church unless it had a Caravaggio or wax statues of celebrities or if they were giving away artisanal jams. Or even just selling them at a deep discount. Essentially, my whole aversion to churches is a pretty hollow edict, but it still felt like I was giving him something by being there.

After a long time, we were escorted into the bishop's office. The bishop sat us down and shook the Mormon's hand and they exchanged pleasantries. The Mormon answered a few questions about how his parents were doing, visibly agitated and trying to be still. Never once was I acknowledged, not even by eye contact.

The bishop was a giant, heaving man in an ill-fitting suit and he sat in the severe parallel slats of light that broke through the blinds of his office's sole window. He addressed my boyfriend by his full name and said, "You haven't been here in quite some time."

"Yeah . . . I know," the Mormon said and I could see him wrestle the guilt down.

The bishop looked at him and then swiveled in his chair like a Bond villain glutted on donuts. Leaning into the shadows and out of view momentarily, we heard him pull open a file cabinet. He retrieved a folder, thumbed through it and found the name he was looking for. He then pulled out a slender dossier containing a few pages of handwritten notes I could not see. That's when things got weird.

"So. What brings you here today?" he asked in a low, menacing drawl, pausing heavily between each word like a honky-tonk Darth Vader, blocked sinuses and all.

The Mormon sighed, folding and unfolding his hands. He was silent for a long moment, looking off with a tight, pained expression, his eyes flitting any direction but the bishop's. He then launched suddenly and fully into the story of how we'd met a year ago, been together, had some ups and downs, broke up, how he met another girl, started seeing her, decided he'd made a mistake, got back together with me and now he had a lot of guilt about what he'd done and wanted some help.

The bishop folded up his sausage fingers but otherwise didn't move one brittle hair through the whole story. For the five or ten minutes it took the Mormon to stutter it all out, the bishop just sat there like a boulder perspiring in the sun and listened with his mean little face all bound up in jowls.

When the Mormon finished and looked down in shame, the bishop stared at him firmly and said, "Have you been fornicating?"

This is when I realized the bishop was full of shit. No insight, no analysis, no compassion. That lack of compassion was the most inexcusable: it didn't matter if we were good together, or if he'd hurt me or hurt himself. There was only one thing that mattered to God, at least as far as the bishop was concerned.

The Mormon nodded slowly and sadly.

"The Lord is very clear in his declaration that sex before marriage is a sin."

The Mormon nodded again, more quickly. They then entered into a conversation about our physical relationship as if I wasn't even in the room. I wish I could say I told the bishop where he should stick his maize, but instead I just sat there in the darkened office listening to this awful man placed unjustly in a position of authority as he questioned my boyfriend about the kind of monogamous, protected sex we were having. I obviously didn't think a Christian bishop was going to let the whole premarital sex thing slide, but I figured there'd be some actual guidance mixed in with the condemnation.

Right about then I began to feel extremely uncomfortable. I suppose it was because a morbidly obese stranger was asking my boyfriend how often we had sex. Even worse, it was only during the more explicit moments that I was acknowledged: the bishop's eyes would edge a little in my direction and I had the distinct impression he was trying to visualize the answers to his questions. He looked at my legs.

The whole conversation was so gross and mortifying that I searched around the office for anything else to think about. I settled on yet another velvet painting—at this point I'm just assuming Joseph Smith didn't care for watercolors—a huge, crudely fashioned diptych. The right side depicted people bathed in God's love, with much light and clouds and flattering white unisex smocks. On the left side, the world was shrouded in darkness and everything was rubble and people were screaming and visibly injured because God had turned away from them and they couldn't have any smocks. One thing I remember most vividly was that the "rubble" depicted was made of both fallen modern-day skyscrapers and a structure that looked like the Acropolis. I wondered if the destruction of the Acropolis was supposed to represent the destruction of logic and reason and hubris or if it was just another example of how Mormon velvet painters have a pretty laissez-faire attitude toward historical accuracy. It also bothered me that everyone in the rubble looked like they were in agony; it seemed pretty awful that God would leave them out like that, in full view of all the cloud frolicking. It was then I decided to never again take shit from any representative of any religion that has to scare people into believing in God. Moreover, I wasn't going to listen to a diatribe about sin from someone who looked like he was hiding a Christmas ham under his Men's Wearhouse jacket. The Lord's also very clear about that.

We left and the Mormon regretted it and only felt worse, which is understandable because in addition to his own remorse he had to deal with this horrible man's judgment. Our relationship dragged out miserably for another year and he seemed to suffer under increasing guilt from all the monogamous, protected sex we continued to have. I finally broke it off and the only thing I really brought out of the relationship was this suspicion that all Christians like lemon squares. I'm being facetious, obviously (Christians love all citrus desserts, not just lemon squares). Apparently after we broke up he met some girl who was really into "erotic knot tying," which is a pretty canny way of coping with your crushing sex guilt.

We weren't right for each other. I'd wager few people can really be "right" for anyone in their early twenties but, in the end, he was a good person. He still is. As for the bishop, I hope he chokes on a lobster roll (something with shellfish). Or maybe autoerotic asphyxiation. He seemed like that kind of guy. You can always tell, like how some people are Beatles people and others like the Stones.

The Mormon and those like him may always be the sort I go for, these men with Christian values who don't believe in God. There's something appealingly complicated about them, but they still open doors for you. Part of me wonders if this is some weird fetish I've developed from an upbringing mostly free of religion.

The other part of me (the part that loves canned statements!) knows it was all worth it because whenever someone asks, "Why were you dating a Mormon?" I can just give 'em this cool sideways grin and say, "He put the fear of God in me," and then I can be content with myself since that's at least marginally funny. Because it's a euphemism for intercourse.

GAY ANXIETY

I didn't realize how skewed my perception of normalness was until I got out of my little liberal enclave and went to college. Mine was kind of an opposing narrative to your average sheltered kid arriving at school and his world opening up, by which I mean I found the world outside my hometown to be dramatically less progressive. The most striking example of this is with respect to the LGBTQ communities.

My father played a lot of tennis and—between you and me—*lesbians fucking love tennis.* They can't get enough of it. Thus my parents' social circles were made up of a lot of lesbian couples and, by extension, a lot of the kids I babysat or tutored were cultured in labs. Most of my family's dinners involved more gay couples than straight ones, so I grew up thinking having two moms was just as normal as anything, if not, statistically speaking, a little more normal.

This, in turn, led to lots of dinner table conversations

involving words like "fag" and "queer," which everyone present were comfortable with because there weren't any doubts about where you stood, politically. My parents' friends all had pretty dark senses of humor and were extremely self-effacing, so I learned to believe that was how you joked as a gay person about being gay.

This means I grew up ascribing absolutely no unflattering qualities to same-sex couples or, at least, none having to do with their sameness. I made fun of our family's gay friends with the same aplomb as I did our family's straight friends. The idea that these people had ever suffered for who they loved or who they fucked was so foreign that it never occurred to me. When Ellen DeGeneres came out on the cover of *Time* with that famously blithe headline (YEP, I'M GAY), I was eleven and couldn't for the life of me understand why that should merit a magazine cover. I consider myself extremely lucky to have grown up in that environment, by which I mean it completely fucked me.

By the time I got to college, casual use of "gay" (and, to an admittedly lesser extent, "fag") were pretty much part of my vocabulary. It turns out they make a lot of people uncomfortable. Because I went to a small, sanctimonious liberal arts college, people were thrilled to take umbrage with those they perceived to be less progressive. They even get kind of competitive over who can be the most outraged. I learned, in about a month, that there are certain words you're not supposed to say unless you are X or Y.

I dropped the words from my vocabulary and got pretty defensive about the idea of being perceived as homophobic in any capacity. For a long time, I didn't even understand how someone could think that about me (in retrospect, it was probably because I said "fag" sometimes). But the problem with that is, once you're worried about being perceived as homophobic, it really shows. You can never go back.

Consequently, whenever I meet a gay person, we always end up talking about their sexuality. The only explanation for this I can imagine is I want to aggressively demonstrate how okay I am with it, which is completely embarrassing and transparent and only puts a focus on their sexuality when it should really have no special place in conversation. Inevitably, when I meet someone who's gay, I always start going on about marriage equality or LGBTQ issues or famous gays who are doing an excellent job of upending gay stereotypes and *holy shit is it awful.*

I start talking about how I grew up in a progressive liberal enclave and thought gay couples were the same as straight couples and how our dinner parties were comprised of more gays than straights and pretty much everything I said, verbatim, a few paragraphs ago. And I use that "lesbians love tennis" joke. Every time. Because really what gays are interested in is a straight perspective on their experience. Moreover, this essay is primarily an agonized exegesis for neurotic, self-loathing liberals because *we need a voice too.* Like *Notes from Underground,* but I say "fag" sometimes.

It gets worse. Because I'm socially awkward, I'll be having this conversation with a gay man, for example, as a straight woman—this conversation about LGBTQ issues—and self-doubt begins to permeate: *Oh my God, seriously? You think he doesn't realize what you're trying to do? You might as well go home and make a crude webcam video about how it's not always going to be so challenging for him then make sure it culminates in you putting duct tape over your mouth and flashing a goddamn peace sign. Post it to Facebook, too. Don't forget to tell him everything you've ever voted for, LGBTQ causes you've given money to and which famous gays you think are really sexually attractive because you're open-minded. Tell him about how sexuality is a spectrum. A spectrum, you know, not binary! Not black and white! Say, "Some people have an extremely literal understanding of sexuality!" It's not patronizing. He's definitely never heard that from an over-compensating hetero asshole before.* This is what my brain does, it starts to turn on itself. It becomes both predator and prey.

Once I've thoroughly patronized him—lesbians love tennis! ha! what an irreverent but obviously not hateful observation!—next begins the part of the conversation where I reverse overcompensate. I start criticizing famous gays and telling this person how I long for high-profile gay men in Hollywood who break the mold of cartoonishly shrill interior decorators. I tell him how I want gay role models for LGBTQ youth who aren't all simpering and one-dimensional, the species of gay that network television has sanitized to the point of glossy asexuality and spoon-fed to middle America, the same ignorants who needed Bill Cosby in order to accept black people. I want a gay's gay! I want famous gays who are stalwart and levelheaded and handsome in conventionally rugged ways. I tell him which gays I think are advanced and "doing important work" and "making a difference." I criticize straight pop stars for arbitrarily declaring themselves gay icons and inserting themselves into gay culture. I act enraged at what I see as the hollowness of their faux solidarity; I suggest that it's merely a shrewd PR move, unintentionally aping my idea of a cynical gay.

The entire time, this hypothetical gay man I'm talking to in a bar is looking at me like, *You complete fucking twat.* As in, do I really think this man—this man who got the shit kicked out of him in middle school, who was made to feel monstrous on account of his instincts, who had to hide his sexuality from his family, who had to rely on shady Internet hookups for gratification, hookups with ostensibly straight men who'd ignore or ridicule him the day after giving him a clandestine BJ in the backseat of a car parked somewhere far removed—do I really think he gives a shit about my opinion on gay culture? Do I really deserve to say anything to this guy?

The reason this even happens, though, is that we're still in a place as a society where some people aren't okay with gays, which is, of course, a gigantic stain on the human race. Homophobia is insidious and therefore a lot of straights like myself find it important to broadcast that we're not among these idiots. Turns out, the only way I can demonstrate fellowship with gays without actually being one is . . . to act like a fucking idiot.

Basically, I am petrified of being confused for a bigot. Which means I'll absolutely be sending this section of the book to all of my gay friends (I have a bunch!) for their explicit approval before it ever sees the light of day—and, sidenote: thank you so much in advance, guys; please let me know if this comes off as callow, reductive and condescending. Hopefully they won't think I've asked for their input purely because of their same-sex preferences—thus defeating my own purpose by abbreviating them to nothing but their sexual orientation in a monumental lack of self-awareness—but that I also respect their opinions because they're so hygienic and well dressed.

When I was in college, my roommates had a friend who was (1) gay and, completely separate from that, (2) insufferable. His gayness had very little to do with his horribleness, although one evening he came over to teach a pole dancing class in the living room and showed invited female attendees how to remove a man's pants with their teeth. I'd find this kind of behavior objectionable in anyone, regardless of gender or sexual preference. He was dumb and loud and abrasive, he had no respect for personal boundaries, he borrowed money he never paid back, all he ever talked about was sex (which, granted, is still a weird objection to make as the author of this book) and he was all around backstabbing, manipulative and bitchy. Essentially, he was everything I disliked about shallow, stupid girls preoccupied with "celeb gossip" and fucking and dieting, only he was a man and therefore I was supposed to overlook all that. Because of his struggle.

I started to hate him after one or two interactions. My roommates, who were both from places that still found gayness very alien, reveled in his affectations. They'd praise his fabulousness, they'd have go-go dancing nights at the club, they'd cherish "girl talk" about red carpet gowns and handsome actors. All the while their friendship developed, I couldn't help but find this behavior more entrenched in homophobia than just about anything I'd seen. They viewed him as nothing more than an over-the-top cliché and it flattered their egos to look past that and embrace him.

This upset me. They didn't treat this guy like a person;

they treated him like a caricature of sexuality that tacitly represented their progressive benevolence. When I started staying in my room while he was over, they couldn't accept that it was because I saw him as a histrionic, self-obsessed liar who participated in conversation only if it was about cock or lean protein. They didn't believe that I disliked his constant, giggly groping. They thought I didn't like him because he was gay. And I would probably be writing this now with at least a leg to stand on, but of course I eventually made a huge ass of myself.

We'll call him Michael, even though he'd actually given himself an outlandish stage name (for his striptease act!) that he expected his friends to call him by. One night, a few friends and I were at the apartment playing a game called Centurion, in which everybody drank a shot of beer once a minute for one hundred minutes, because college is stupid. I was recently recovering from the first split with our Mormon friend and was never really a beer drinker, so I tried matching them (every five minutes) with gin. I don't drink gin anymore.

About forty minutes in, Michael showed up with one of the roommates who wasn't participating and I figured I was drunk enough to tolerate him. I was wrong. Michael immediately launched into a terrible diatribe about a mutual female friend who—he suspected—had gained some weight and he didn't understand why she figured she could still "get away with" short skirts. He called her "thunder thighs," and said she needed to consume nothing but "celery and laxatives" for the forseeable future. The sober roommate giggled and giggled because wasn't it funny how he was being such a bitch!

But really, no, he was being hateful and misogynist and she permitted it because it was his shtick.

After the game, by which time I'd become completely obliterated and deeply irritated, the sober roommate wanted to drive to an on-campus party. We all piled into the car, with Michael in the front seat and the four of us wasted Centurions in the back. After a few minutes, a terrible motion sickness began to sink in and all I could hear was Michael being a dick from the front seat. Because my brain was wrecked by alcohol, I said, "God this is so gay."

Everyone went kind of quiet.

"No, I'm sorry. This is gay. Riding in the back of . . . the cars . . . when you're this drunk is . . . for gay people."

I could see Michael's shocked expression in the rearview as he met eyes with the driver and I was spurred to continue.

"No, listen Michael, I respeck your lifestyle. I do. I respecked it. But this is fucking gay."

I think, at the time, I was so wasted that this was my idea of irony, insofar as I was trying to be a parody of a heterosexual in much the same way I thought he was a parody of mainstream gay culture. I guess I was trying to match him in cartoonish behavior that reduced my sexual orientation to a caricature as thinly drawn and stupidly conceived as his own: a patronizing, sanctimonious idiot who still used that language pejoratively.

This is, of course, what I thought was happening and that I was being very clever. But it wasn't what was actually happening. Regardless of what I thought or how impressed with my own meta-joke I was, my behavior was nothing more than a stupid confluence of my comfort with using "gay" as a put-down and feelings of paranoia that my roommates thought I disliked him on account of his sexuality. This was not the alcohol's fault; obviously it was mine. For this, I do feel shame, that even as a bleeding heart I still managed to hurt him and use effectively homophobic language in doing so, against this person who not more than a year before had been hospitalized by people who didn't appreciate his simpering affectations either. I regret the whole thing, whether or not he was a total asshole. The next thing I remember is vomiting in a trash can that I'd pulled into a bathroom stall (?) and the campus drunk questioning me through the door with comical apprehension, "Are you sure you're okay?" and this was an eerie moment of clarity.

The next day, when I woke up at four p.m., my roommates were sitting in a quiet circle in the living room, waiting for me. They confronted me about the night before and I lied and said I didn't remember a word of it. They were furious because Michael had said he wasn't coming over anymore because of my homophobia and I think—somewhere deep down—even they realized he was overreacting. But they were still going to punish me for it. One of the roommates never really forgave me for the whole thing and tensions ran pretty high for the rest of the year. That roommate eventually moved in with Michael. He ended up owing her a few months' rent and skipping town. She never saw him again but apparently never admitted she thought he was a bad person, because that was inconsistent with her ideas about herself.

I learned a valuable lesson about using those words. But before I say a little more about that, I want to add that I've heard a lot of arguments for why everyone should be able to say a word like "faggot." One is a backlash to political sensitivity frequently made by stand-up comedians; on a really obvious level, sometimes the best way to mock a genuinely stupid mindset—like that belonging to a bigot—is to mimic their reasoning and expose its absurdity, and in so doing we employ words like "faggot," "homo," and so on. I once heard a high school football player call another a "gay homo queer fag," which you just can't make up and shouldn't die in obscurity because it's perfect.

I've heard a lot of people justify using "faggot" by insisting it doesn't mean "one who is attracted to those of the same gender," that instead "faggot" actually means asexual and pathetic and feeble, that a "fag" is just someone who's a whiny bitch. A twerp. Which is uncomfortably dubious because this definition is the same as our old primitive misconceptions about gay men, that one's sexuality has something to do with one's *manliness* (which itself assumes that manliness is somehow an important quality). I've never quite been persuaded by people who claim that "gay" or "fag" are acceptable pejoratives because they just mean weak and helpless and asexual. Then again, as the old saying goes, "All babies are faggots until they fuck something."

I see no justification for using a word like "fag" to mean pathetic because individual pursuit and knowledge of what one wants—especially in the face of judgment from others—is practically heroic. I am lucky to be of an orientation not oppressed by bigots and simpletons, but I have an abiding admiration for people resolute enough to know what they want, or to try to find out. I had a friend in college who was a straight man; one night, he took up a gay friend's offer of a blowjob just to see if he was into men. In other words, he took a heuristic approach to his sexuality. He then explained what had happened to a keg party full of men not an hour after. Though all the other guys made fun of him ruthlessly, I was in awe. I thought he was the Niels Bohr of getting blown by a dude.

After the incident in the car, I felt the responsible thing would be to expunge those words from my vocabulary. They weren't necessary. It wasn't about my "right" to use them, even in attempts at satire; it was about not being a shitty person. I never wanted to be thought of as homophobic, strange though the idea was. I didn't even want to be thought of as cruel.

Lucky for me, though, I landed in the best loophole imaginable when I started dating a man who used to fuck men. Not just fuck them, mind you, but also have meaningful long-term relationships with them. This was a non-issue for us because (sorry for being an asshole) I actually do believe sexuality is a spectrum; I just happen to fall in a very boring place on it. He falls in the middle. One thing that attracted me most to him was his lack of fear of other people and his upbringing and his Midwestern peers while trying to figure out what he wanted. I tend to go for men who'd probably benefit from a little sporting exploration; he's the only one who actually followed through and ironed out who he was.

Moreover, I can say "faggot" forever. Forever. It's like how people in interracial relationships can say mind-blowingly racist things to each other to get rises out of people but no one can ever accuse them of being actually racist because they're in love and they hold hands and have a joint savings account and fuck each other a lot. Much in this way, I can't be a bigot because I'm with a man who's been in love with men. Which would make me a pretty incompetent bigot, if I was one. I'll have to stop immediately if we ever break up, but I'm holding out that we'll stay together and have lots of self-impressed little babies. And, once they're old enough, we'll be able to joke in ways that their peers with boring hetero parents could never imagine: I'll do all kinds of hilarious impressions like "mommy learning to toss a salad properly" and "mommy trying to put her hands in daddy's asshole like his ex-boyfriend used to," and then I'll make all these exaggerated expressions of confusion and I'll shrug and sigh and it'll be like a Charlie Chaplin movie (but we'll say "fag" sometimes).

SO YOU'VE CAUSED AN ABORTION

The manner in which I first encountered abortion was, strangely, the same way most adolescent boys discover porn: late at night on the Internet. I was about twelve and had been introduced to a website over Thanksgiving dinner, by one of the older female cousins not scandalized by the sex tape I found. My family, as you've probably deduced, is fond of black humor and my cousin had a particularly morbid proclivity. She told me about all the grotesque images you'd find on this website, then produced a laptop and showed me a few. The one that stuck out was a man who'd died in his bathtub while the water was running really hot and it roiled around his corpse for a few days, resulting in what can only accurately be described as man soup. Unless stew is technically more accurate? Whichever one is meat-based.

Enthused by this trove of objectionable things suddenly available to me, I went home that night and started down the rabbit hole of primitive Internet perversity. Websites full of bodies, generally dead by some gruesome misfortune, led to websites of violent urban legends and ghost stories and animal abuse hoaxes (like putting kittens in different shaped glasses to grow funnily shaped kittens) and dead baby jokes and so on. That first night, I was hunched over my computer very late, unable to resist all the appalling descriptions, clicking them and trying to assess the gore of a half-loaded image through cracked fingers.

One such option claimed to show "the victims of abortion," and, not knowing what that was, I clicked through. The initial text I don't recall very well; it might have been a parody of religious right rhetoric or it might have been blatantly irreverent, I can't remember. What I do remember, however, was (1) discovering what an abortion was and (2) the visual component.

I had stumbled on an endless column of abortion aftermath. Gleaming trays of red medical waste speckled with identifiably human parts: half-formed eyeballs, hands, feet, lobes of head and sprouting ears. Some abortions are performed on clusters of cells; others on little beings. These were the kind you recognized.

Here's the thing, though: you can't really gauge the size of an aborted fetus just by eyeballing it; you need something set beside it. Thanks to the site's morally bankrupt hosts, the increment of measurement was . . . a SpaghettiO. Someone had digitally added stacked circles of the popular canned ring pasta on top of images of expelled fetuses *for scale*. What made this even more impressively ghastly was that—when digitally added on top of an image of an aborted fetus—SpaghettiOs kind of blend.

Soon after, I became a teenager and my ignorant teenage brain eagerly sought any argument that made the noises of intellectual activity. I, embarrassingly, spent a lot of conversations about reproductive rights saying that I supported abortion on a case by case basis and that "women who use abortions as birth control" are monstrous, immoral sluts. I was sixteen.

This contrarian narcissism eventually took the shape of indifference: I didn't think much about abortion because I wasn't the "kind" of person who'd get one. This common but no less stupid assumption wasn't terribly hard to understand: I'd never needed one and none of my friends ever talked about having one. As a person who had always been neurotic to the point of obsession about safe sex, I genuinely believed abortion was the dominion of the less responsible, the unsympathetic. What's impressive is that I managed to believe such a thing for so long.

This is especially impressive considering I went to college at a pretty busy time for sexual politics: people were feeling less and less ashamed of what they wanted and more empowered to get it. By which I really mean, yes, there is organic lubricant; yes, there are manifold cock ring options for you if you're allergic to rubber; absolutely there is body chocolate without preservatives. If you'd like to buy a vibrator, there is a store on Main Street that's as futuristically soulless as an Asian fusion restaurant and, if you want, you can even get one with a little twirling dolphin on it and I don't know who likes dolphins that much but those people are apparently out there in droves. Further, no matter how strange and dark and off you think you are, there is already an active online community for your strange dark offness, if not extensive communities writing erotica specifically focused on it. I'd wager we're maybe a year off the availability of small-batch edible underwear.

This world of increasing sexual liberation still runs up against the old thing: the shame and the confusion and the tragic lack of education. Sometimes they collide. One consequence of this is that once someone blamed me for an abortion they got.

My college had two campuses on different sides of the country and intercampus transfer was encouraged; I decided to do two years in New Mexico and then spent the next two in Maryland. Early in my junior year, I was thus in Maryland, sitting at a wrought-iron table under the hum of cicadas in dense humidity as the first big campus-wide party of the year took place (it occurred on both campuses, like most of the major parties). I'd always hated the party in question: it was an opulent, vulgar excuse for everyone to dress up in costume and act really, really college. The conceit was that the freshmen wore virginal whites and the sophomores, juniors and seniors wore black (the administration wore a blind eye). The party was about "seducing and corrupting" the poor freshmen and their whites enabled predatory upperclassmen to do so. Weirdly, if there's one thing I learned from my four years in private liberal arts education, it's that people love drinking in funny outfits. It never occurs to anyone they're going to be paying off debts for untold years just so they can enjoy four brief ones as an alcoholic in costume.

I was having a cigarette outside on the quad—at one of the tables blanketed in condoms by the decoration committee—when some people I knew came along and sat down. We had been there for about twenty minutes when we noticed two white-clad kids on a stone bench beneath a magnolia tree, kissing hungrily. We watched them for a little while because the outsized physicality and showmanship of their lust was hilarious. They appeared to have met at most a few hours before, likely less, and were obviously about to make some terrible decisions together. We, at the average age of twenty, sat there smug in our wisdom.

One of the kids with me was a guy named Sandeep, who'd nicknamed me Axl Rose on account of my messy shag haircut. While watching the two freshmen grope and slobber on each other, Sandeep decided to take advantage of my look. He began by announcing I wasn't actually as cool as Axl Rose, which of course caught my attention.

"Axl Rose," he said, "would walk over to those two freshmen and hand them a condom."

Now sober, I can say with complete certainty that Axl Rose *would not.*

He went on about how Axl Rose was so rock 'n' roll and would totally go over and interrupt their lusftul motions for his own entertainment. As I have no social skills and struggle to make friends, I became immediately embarrassed and admitted I would never be as cool as Axl Rose and it would be great if they all stopped looking at me immediately.

Another kid, a rich WASP from Manhattan who drove an Aston Martin, chimed in that he'd pay twenty bucks to see it.

Sandeep thought for a minute and added Axl Rose would be so brash as to sit down on the male freshman's lap and hand him the condom that way.

The WASP added: "Forty dollars."

Sandeep—rumored to have paid his way through college by online poker playing and a bit of a betting man—raised the stakes: in order to be as cool as Axl Rose and make sixty dollars off of this, I'd need to walk over to the underclassmen, sit down on the guy's lap, hand him a condom and whisper in his ear, "Seal the deal." He swiped up a random condom from the pile on the table and held it out expectantly.

Let me tell you about my financial situation in college: I spent most weekday nights studying and most weekend afternoons working at an outdoor apparel store so I could afford groceries (I eventually moved on to waiting tables). I still have no idea why I was hired at a store that traded in ski and sailing jackets; in my initial interview I was asked to list my favorite outdoor activities, and through a mixture of interview anxiety, misguided irreverence and possibly Asperger's, I said, "Smoking." The man who hired me must have taken it as a joke because soon I was peddling sailing shoes and fleeces to barrel-chested power boaters with hundred-thousand-dollar watches. This way, I scrounged together enough to afford cans of tuna, microwaveable soups and tea, while the rest went to paying for a cab to the nearest grocery store, a twenty-minute drive away. This potential sixty-dollar windfall represented unspeakable opulence: cheeses, mixed nuts, grocery store sushi, beef jerky, dried fruit, bell peppers! To provide a more succinct portrait of how broke I was then, right around that time I saw a man walking down the street eating two Twix bars side by side out of the wrapper—*as if they were one candy bar*—and I thought it was the truest expression of luxury I had ever seen.

Needless to say, I sat down on that stranger's lap and whispered in his ear, "Seal the deal," as he looked at me bewildered through his glasses and accepted the condom seemingly only to ensure I go away. It was perhaps the most uncharacteristic thing I have ever done.

A year and a half later—amid those indescribable last few months of college that are equally fraught with doubt, accomplishment and restlessness—I was at a friend's party and waiting in line for the bathroom. Standing there, probably thinking about nothing, I was approached suddenly in the hallway by a kid I'd never seen before. Before I knew it, he'd backed me against a wall with his finger between my eyes. I'm not normally one to be frightened of shorter people but aggressive pointing makes me uncomfortable.

"You," he growled, "you owe me a pack of cigarettes." He was a chubby kid, with delicately styled facial hair and a scarf piled *just so* around his shoulders. He looked like someone who always kept a notepad on his person to scribble down bits of poetry when they struck him. He was also swaying where he stood.

I blinked, his index finger pressed just above the bridge of my nose, and said, "Who are you?"

"You don't remember me?" He looked shocked, the kind you get when the shock is so thorough it becomes an insult.

"I have no idea who you are," I said. I just needed to use the bathroom.

"You don't? You really don't?" He got even closer.

"Nope."

He said through gritted teeth, "You ruined my life."

Here I felt a faint recognition. Didn't he work in the coffee shop downtown . . . ? "Are you the guy from—"

He snorted. "You gave me a condom and said, 'Seal the deal.' "

"Oh yeah!"

"I used it that night with the girl you saw me with. I made the worst mistake of my life."

I probably had the decency to grimace here, because I did understand he was alluding to having sex and some kind of attendant consequences.

"You ruined my life."

"Whoa—" I said and paused.

"Phillip," he offered.

"Phillip. You had sex and *I* ruined your life?" And my brain immediately set to thinking, *I made sixty dollars off that! What did I buy with the money? I bet it was good. Beef jerky? Cashews? Yogurt? The good kind of yogurt?*

"The condom broke."

My jaw dropped.

For the first time, he broke eye contact. He said, "We didn't keep it."

The thought that came into my head was one of horror: *I bought SpaghettiOs.*

He looked at me again and his expression was not all anguish but instead a kind of drunken contempt. "I dropped out of school. I work in a coffee shop now."

For obvious reasons, I was unsure what to say.

"We didn't know what the fuck we were doing," he said. "I

was . . . I'd never used a condom before"—the finger hovered up again but he didn't stick it between my eyes—"so you owe me a pack of cigarettes."

This was a lot to take in. "Why do I owe you a pack of cigarettes?"

"Because you owe me something and I'm a little drunk. And I don't have any cigarettes. And you do. So I want you to give me one of yours right now, and then I want you to buy me a pack of Pall Malls later. Unfilteredsss," he slurred.

I was beginning to suspect this was some elaborate performance. "I owe you a pack of cigarettes because a girl you were with got an abortion?"

"Yes."

"And you've set the value of your unborn child's life at . . . twenty-one cigarettes? And the brand of the twenty-first one doesn't matter?"

"Yes."

"That doesn't make any sense."

"Of course it makes sense. You ruined my life and I want cigarettes and you have them. And you're going to buy me some because I had to drop out of college and work at a fucking coffee shop."

"I'm not the reason you work in a coffee shop. Also, you can't arbitrarily pick something for me to owe you."

He looked outraged. "So you're not going to buy me cigarettes?"

"No. Me buying you cigarettes would be an admission of guilt." Even still, I was impressed by his willingness to make such a disturbing claim to a stranger at a party who was trying to use a bathroom.

He started again, "I don't know how you can be such a callous bitch after what I've told you," but then his strange, accusatory aggression swept away and he looked overcome. It was about here I realized he was *extremely* drunk. "Before that," he said and came out with it, "I was a virgin. That was the worst mistake of my life. You ruined my life."

It was about here that the initial swell of empathy in my heart just went away, because abortion, like divorce, is a shitty thing that's usually for the best. The only thing sadder than some eighteen-year-olds misusing a condom and tearing it somehow and one of them having to go get an abortion was the idea of this drunk idiot being a father. That unborn baby practically owed me a favor (in a roundabout way).

"I'm sorry, Phillip, but I'm not going to buy you cigarettes."

"I'm sorry you're such a bitch."

I looked at him flatly because I couldn't quite discern if any of this was true (or even happening) but just then the door to the bathroom opened. Before ducking inside, I said, "Excuse me, my water broke." Which in retrospect was pretty raw.

'm still conflicted about the confrontation, though I can identify the big flaw in Phillip's logic: even though I had given him the condom, I was only one link in a chain of culpability. If Phillip could lay the blame on me, then I could easily lay the blame on Sandeep, who handed me the condom in the first place. But Sandeep got a pass, too, because he could blame whatever anonymous decorating committee member who had dumped the condoms on the table. The anonymous decorating committee member would be well within his or her rights to blame the manufacturer for the defective product. Moreover, myself, Sandeep, the Manhattan WASP with the Aston Martin, the anonymous decorating committee member, and the manufacturer would all be invited to comfortably blame Axl Rose as the architect of this whole abortion kerfuffle. Why stop there when we've yet to include cheap beer, my hairstylist and how inarguably great *Appetite for Destruction* is? Similarly, if someone hands you a gun, and you shoot yourself, are they responsible? That depends. There's probably actual case law about this. Let's just say if the person who hands you the gun is legally responsible, they shouldn't be. However, one factor that, without question, did contribute to the abortion was drunken sex between teenagers.

All those other factors could have been different, but the outcome of the situation was still ultimately determined by decisions made by two people to have sex. Sex has consequences. If they aren't adequately explained to people, systematically and starting at a very young age, they go around making stupid decisions without ever comprehending the negative results. Which brings me to the most important thing we could possibly talk about once we all agree that nobody wants an abortion: you can't get enough sex ed.

I'm going to make a pretty unfair, unfounded assumption here (this is my book) and say that Phillip probably wasn't endowed with a terrific sex education. I'm basing that on his inability to really accept responsibility for the consequences of his actions and also I think he was from Mississippi. Of course eighteen-year-olds can't accept responsibility for the consequences of sex if they aren't properly terrified of them.

There's an allegorical argument for sex ed (and all ed, for

that matter) in the Bible. The argument appears in Genesis, when God tells Adam and Eve not to eat from the Tree of Knowledge. God commands, "Ye shall not eat of it, neither shall ye touch it, lest ye die." Basically he just says, "Don't eat the pears, they're poisonous," and then he leaves them be, expecting them not to want to eat pears ever, even though they're used to having all of their wishes fulfilled all the time. That is abstinence-only education: "Don't do it. It'll kill you. Don't ask questions." Eventually, Eve meets the serpent and the serpent says, "I ate it and I'm not dead. *And* it gave me the gift of speech." The serpent (seemingly) is a living, breathing, talking demonstration of God being wrong with regard to the fruit's fatalness. In this way, the serpent represents every other message kids receive about sex: "It's not dangerous at all. It's just awesome."

Alternatively, if God had said, "Well, it's not lethal per se, insofar as it won't kill you immediately. It's more like it's going to give you this fleeting thrill but then there's going to be all kinds of darkness that descends on you and you're going to be ashamed of your bodies and you're not going to be able to communicate telepathically with animals anymore. You'll be cast out of the garden and then you'll have to toil over a hard land in shadows until your hands bleed—also, you'll bleed and that's its own separate horror—and then, after a long tedious life of labor and resentment and self-loathing and murderous, megalomaniacal children, your bones will become frail and your skin will sag off your body and you'll be unrecognizable to yourself. *Then* you'll die. So, when I say the fruit will 'kill' you, I'm not describing an immediate physical death, it's more of a protracted spiritual death in concert with a long, agonized slide toward physical death. Does that make sense? Do you have any questions?"

If God had presented things this way—that is, as a comprehensive breakdown of the consequences that would befall them if they ate from the Tree—Eve might have been able to critically evaluate the serpent's claims. In this way, original sin is a beautiful, probably unintentional argument for why we should give kids good sex education: they might still go after the pears, but at least it's an informed decision. If we tell them about herpes and warts and crabs and syphilis and burning pee and pregnancy and AIDS, they'll be that much less reckless when it comes to sex. Or, we could just cryptically tell them not to have it.

I left the party with the impression that Phillip was a drunk, ornery teenager who couldn't take responsibility for his actions. If I thought about it at all in the next few days, it was with a baffled awe that anyone would behave that way. I figured he was telling the truth, at least, because it made more sense than him trying to accumulate free cigarettes with the old you-caused-my-abortion con. I didn't really think about what he'd gone through or why he was angry. I didn't think about what a terrifying thing unwanted pregnancy is to a young person. I had always been responsible.

Right after graduation, my then-boyfriend and I stayed at his parents' house in upstate New York. We were living out of his childhood bedroom while we looked for a place in Brooklyn, taking the bus down and staying with friends as we marched through the demoralizing nightmare that is trying to find a New York apartment on the Internet with no clue what New York is like.

I had always kept birth control next to my toothbrush, so I could take it at the same time every day. Just like I had since I was fifteen, years before I became sexually active, as prescribed to me by a dermatologist. Unfortunately, my then-boyfriend's parents were remarkably good at lying to themselves about the grown-up habits of their grown-up son. For example, he'd smoked for years but did so on late-night walks, far enough away to ensure they couldn't see the cherry of a lit cigarette in his hands. When he got his yearly STD tests, he checked the mail compulsively for days, to ensure his parents did not suss out the dark truth that he was being a responsible adult. There was no way I could just keep my birth control in plain sight in the bathroom, though I felt that was perfectly fair.

Unfortunately, with my birth control hidden deep in my luggage, I was having trouble remembering to take it at the same time every day. Toward the end of the month, I forgot a day and then another day and then I was late. The first two nights were a private panic, in which I hoped things were just off and didn't want to involve my then-boyfriend in the anxiety under which I was squirming.

On the third day, the terror was looming too high to ignore. I admitted to my then-boyfriend that I was late and fearful I was pregnant. In my desperation, I asked him if we could keep it, if he'd even be open to that. He said no. We went to the store and bought a pregnancy test.

Soon, I was sitting alone in the bathroom, on the floor next to the magazine rack, trying to build up some courage and take the test. His father—who might charitably be described as a vain, socially inept academic—stocked the bathroom with one kind of reading material: scientific journals in which he'd been published. His father was impressed only by scholarly accomplishments (especially his own) so they were scattered all over the house to remind my then-boyfriend of his inadequacies. Staring at that magazine bin full of testaments to his father's achievement, my first thoughts were of the judgment I'd face if we could not keep my hypothetical abortion secret. I would be a stain on the family if I killed their unborn grandson, who could have been a proper scholar and gotten published in the same journals. I would be depriving them of progeny they'd admire more.

Inevitably, my thoughts turned to my then-boyfriend's mother, the woman whose favorite game was Telling Stories About All the Girls My Son Has Known Who Are Better Than You, progenitor of the Laura from High School fable. I would never be the Ivy League–educated architect or lawyer or art history major that I needed to be in order to impress her; I would just be this. She wouldn't be bragging about me to anyone anyway, but now she'd just be quiet and not even mention me. She'd never brandish Ashley Who Got an Abortion at any of his future girlfriends.

This is a roundabout way of saying that what pervaded my fear so much more than I ever could have anticipated was shame. The casual, flippant rationalizing with which I'd deflected and dismissed Phillip abandoned me; I didn't remember the jokes on the Internet or the ridiculousness of the evening with the condom or Phillip at all. I was too stricken with terror to think of anything but what a brutal mess I'd suddenly been shoved into. When I unsheathed the pregnancy test, I meticulously folded the wrapper up like an origami scarlet letter and buried it in my pocket, afraid that someone would root through the trash can looking for evidence of my transgressions.

A strange clarity came over me when I was confronted with the thing itself. There was the pregnancy test, naked in my hands, as ominously preposterous as a crystal ball . . . and it was then I experienced my first full, lucid, rational thought in several minutes: *I should really stockpile these.*

Turns out, when you're ashamed and terrified that you might need an abortion, the last thing you want to do is go to Walgreens. For one, they don't offer them there.

I was deathly still for a long time—or what felt like a long time, sitting on a bathroom floor and suspicious there was an unwanted entity inside of me. Then the terrible thinking began: I was three years into a relationship, had just graduated college and was going to move to New York City to try to get a book published. I had all these ideas about my hopes and dreams and how to realize them: contacts I had and favors I could beg out of people, how I was going to wait tables four nights a week and work on my novel for the other three, non-stop, all day. How I'd been working for that my whole life, how I'd go to New York City and live somewhere cool and gritty and get a book deal. I didn't think it was going to be two hundred pages of facile revelations about men I've allowed inside of me, but it takes forty-three muscles to frown and probably less to make a cheap joke about vaginal odor.

I had all of these things I was working for and was going to achieve and I'd just finished college and that was going to help me somehow, too. I realize that if this isn't a concise expression of my privilege then nothing is, but I thought about this when convinced I was pregnant because my first instinct amid the confusion and fear was to keep it. Perhaps some of that was the dread and disgust with which I associated abortion, but there was something else. I considered all that I'd accomplished and all that I would and I thought my relationship with the man who would become the father was stable enough and that we had enough money or we'd find the money and we were both going to get good jobs and be hugely successful and have health insurance and an extra bedroom and, until then, both our parents would help us. And that we would try. And if I thought hard enough, I could convince him this was true.

Then I thought, *Why would I give up everything so I can provide a shitty life to something else?*

It was crazy. Why would I trash all my aspirations to spend the rest of my life trying to provide for a child I didn't plan for and didn't want? Not only that, the would-be father would be a terrible father and the would-be grandparents would barely contain their derision. My own parents would be so disappointed in me because they didn't work hard to put me through college just so I could graduate and a month later get knocked up and spend the rest of my life suffocating under student loans as I toiled to provide for what was, at that moment, not an adorable baby but probably nothing more than imperceptible biological function performing itself inside of me. A blip of primordial red ooze. Not even a SpaghettiO.

Not only all of that but the whole mundane hassle of securing an abortion appalled me: I hate phone calls, for one. I hate waiting rooms. I hate waiting at all because I'm naturally very punctual. I hate *Highlights* magazine and I hate co-pays. I hated every conceivable thing about the idea of scheduling and procuring an abortion, hiding it from his parents, living with no small guilt—or it least the nagging recognition of it—forever, but maybe more than anything, I hated having to suffer the bottomless indignity of staring at Jennifer Aniston's *fucking face* from the cover of a celebrity weekly while under oppressive fluorescent light in some cold, unfeeling anteroom as I waited to have my insides scraped out by a stranger while I remained awake.

I looked at the plastic in my hands and thought to myself, *Well, I hope I don't have to do this.*

It was then, before I even took the test, that I came to terms with how I actually felt about abortion: I abandoned every argument and affectation and faux-provocative stance I'd ever had because the truth of the matter was I would get one, too, if I needed it. Suddenly those anonymous, irresponsible sluts looked a lot like me—those straw women who appear in punditspeak, lying back on the operating table with the same blank indifference they'd wear while lying back to be inseminated. I hoped with every fiber of my stupid forgetful being that I was not pregnant. Then I took the test and I wasn't. Because I was lucky.

It's worth noting that my then-boyfriend, who flatly dismissed the idea of raising our hypothetical unwanted child, would years later sit in a bar among a group of male friends and declare that abortion is "not a constitutional right." I'd like to underscore the menacing ease of his morality. This is a convenient stance when one has never had to look at a pregnancy test and wonder what it will say.

I probably would have met Phillip's bizarre intrusion with a bit more sympathy, had my own scare happened just two months before. Even though I still would have found it absurd to use abortions offensively (like a potato gun), I at least would have understood that look on his face. I managed to go from pretty flippant about something to pretty intimately aware of the purpose it serves. It needs to exist, for a litany of reasons, not the least of which is that ladies are human beings and not just incubators you can fuck.

Even though my pregnancy scare revealed to me how I felt about abortion, I'm still pretty ambivalent about Phillip. What happened to him was terrible; what happened to the girl he slept with was terrible. But I feel no guilt, as I imagine Axl Rose does not. Maybe I feel no guilt because there were hundreds of condoms enveloping campus that night and I just happened to be handed a defective one. Maybe I feel no guilt because the condom was perfectly fine until he slipped it on wrong and it ripped. Maybe because he was dumb, drunk, eighteen and about to have sex for the first time and didn't know what he was doing but he was sure as hell doing it. Maybe because I don't believe others can ever be held accountable for the actions of a free-thinking adult individual. Maybe I feel no guilt because I'm a bad person. Or maybe I just think of it as an ethical wash because I made sixty dollars and could buy groceries, meaning one human life was extinguished so another could burn that much brighter. I guess we'll never know.

LIFE IS AN EVIL

I moved to New York a month after college. I wanted to go there my whole life. Growing up, New Agey Californians would regard my black clothes and tightly wound disposition and tell me I belonged in New York City. It always flattered me.

The thing about this city, though, is it corrupts your understanding of what's normal and what's acceptable. There's the obvious sense, that people dress like fashion victims or feel comfortable expressing their sexuality or that we're all spoiled, entitled elitists all the time, such that the second you get out of New York, all you do is complain about the lack of restaurants, cheap and efficient public transportation, museums and live shows, and what time the bars close—all the stuff you take for granted when you live in New York, where anything is actually possible and eventually you can network your way into a book deal. But it does age you; it grinds you down. They say if you want to love New York, you have to leave it a lot. On the bright side, the longer you live here, the better you can play Have You Ever Fucked a Famous Person?

New York isn't special because of all the things about it that have eroded or are eroding as the influx of people like me (and presumably you) continues; what's special about New York is you will see things there, things you could never have imagined. Unspeakable things. Not the man in Union Square dressed as Boba Fett playing the accordion or the man peeling carrots in a three-piece suit in hundred-degree heat (RIP). Not the man who walks around the Village with the cat sitting on his head or the man who drives through Williamsburg in a Subaru, aimlessly and for hours, with all his windows rolled down as he sings Bobby Darin or Frank Sinatra at the top of his lungs. Every weekend. These things are all wonderful but extremely commonplace. I'm talking about the dark stuff.

As you know, New York consists of five boroughs: Manhattan, Brooklyn, Queens, the Bronx and Staten Island. Many would call that order of importance. I live in Brooklyn, for lack of imagination and love of small batches, but also (I'm being serious) I very much dislike crowds. Manhattanites like to hate on Brooklyn because the legacy of New York as we know it was shaped primarily in Manhattan. Of course, what they're ignoring is that everything that makes New York City great is slowly migrating outward in tandem with rising rents. You can't really fall back on the legacy of Max's Kansas City, the Velvet Underground, sixties Bohemianism, punk and Patti Smith, hip-hop and Rothko and *The Recognitions*, New Wave and the Harlem Renaissance, queer culture and Woody Allen and *Some Girls*, five-for-a-dollar dumplings and every band you care about and *Harper's Magazine,* club comics and Andy Warhol and falafel and getting murdered—all that stuff could never have happened with Manhattan costing as much as it does now.

Also, the argument is invalid for this simple reason: Manhattan is not "more" New York than any other borough because, by that logic, some shitty trust-fund kid who lives in a gaudy palace on the Upper East Side would then be considered "more" New York than an aging teamster from Queens (reductio ad absurdum). Further, the Wu-Tang Clan is from Staten Island, Run-DMC and A Tribe Called Quest are from Queens, and MCA and Biggie were from Brooklyn.

What I'm trying to say is that every borough of New York has amazing things to offer (or, at least, I've heard that there's a really good Indian restaurant in Staten Island) and they all need to accept that. I don't think any one borough has more than the others and I think pitting them against each other is stupid—especially when all the good Thai food is in Queens—but what I will say is this: you see way more exposed genitals in Manhattan than anywhere else. As much as people like to say that Manhattan is the civilized, wealthy borough—the gated community of New York's art-buying, garage-having elite—I have seen one hundred percent of my pre–nine a.m. dicks on the streets of Manhattan. And if I have learned anything from walking around the island it's this: if you see a person who seems like he's got his dick in his hands or has something crazy issuing from his nose or face, don't look closer.

The absolute most horrifying thing I have ever seen in New York—and everyone has their story—occurred on a little tree-lined street in the Greenpoint neighborhood of Brooklyn, a quiet, clean street that would probably be very appealing to people with kids if all the houses weren't covered in vinyl siding.

It must have been about eight in the morning and I was walking to work. So it happened that I was ambling down this little street, worrying about stupid work things, and ahead of me, about two-thirds of the way up the block, I saw this guy lying on his back. His knees were bent and in the air, he had his toes just touching the edge of the sidewalk. From where I was, I could just make out that he was holding something up to his face.

I figured, *There he is under a tree, in front of a car, maybe he's trying to take photos from extreme angles of his Corolla.*

Nothing yet seemed out of the ordinary. People like sharing banalities on the Internet and taking photographs of lame shit so people with whom they attended second grade can see the lame shit they're currently looking at.

But I kept walking closer and began to think to myself, *That guy has a pretty intense blowout! He looks like he's on a reality television show about people who get into fistfights.* He was wearing one of those silly shirts that horrible men wear that have tattoos and flair built into them because I guess getting actual barbwire tattoos is too much of a commitment but you still want the look. I'm also pretty sure he was wearing snap-away pants, which are acceptable only if you are ten years old and in the nineties, walking onto a kickball field and the world is moving in lushly hallucinogenic slow motion around you. He looked like he'd been out all night before, knocking back sixteen-dollar-a-pop rail vodka Red Bull at some awful club,

which is to say definitely not a homeless person. At this point
I could see that he wasn't holding a camera and his hands were
not steady like someone taking pictures, but bouncing up and
down over his mouth.

I got about ten feet away and I heard a noise, a shrill
smacking noise. It was very loud. I started getting curious
about what this guy lying on the sidewalk at eight in the
morning was doing.

Maybe he's eating ribs?

Illogical.

. . . Breakfast ribs?

Even though this was a small, quiet, mostly residential
neighborhood in North Brooklyn, the morning commute had
long begun and people were coming down their stoops and
shutting car doors and talking on cell phones around cigarettes, I could barely hear any of it. It was all drowned out by
this full wet smacking noise.

My common sense usually kicks in, now that I've lived in
New York for a couple years, but this time it just fucking
abandoned me. About two feet away, I glanced down against
my better judgment.

It was right then I finally saw what he was holding: the
body of a dead baby bird. His hands were about three or four
inches apart and I could see its sad little unformed wings
spread between them. He was jangling it over his mouth.

Breakfast ribs were pretty much out at this point. So I
thought, *Perhaps he is trying to resuscitate that dead baby bird in
a strikingly unsanitary fashion?*

Just as I was walking over him, I saw the dead baby bird's
head lolling around uselessly. I guess it was the sight of its

shriveled little face that made it all dawn on me. The jangling of its body fell into terrible, gruesome step with the noisy smacking sound he was making with his mouth and I knew in this clear moment on this bright morning, rushing to the subway but paused there and captivated—he was sucking on its butt.

It was as though I became separate from myself, like in moments of trauma when people see their bodies from above. I looked down and I understood and I kept moving because that's the survival instinct New York crushes into you, even if you're a fearful kid from Wine Country. I looked down and I saw what I saw and my quiet reaction was equivalent to thinking to myself, *Huh.*

It wasn't until about an hour later that the truth of the matter all dawned on me. It wasn't even when I was on the subway. It wasn't until I got to work and sat down in front of my computer and saw my own reflection in the darkened screen that it hit me: *That guy with the stiff blowout is lying on the sidewalk trying to orally pleasure a dead baby bird.*

Only in New York!

PORN STAR PROBLEMS

I moved to New York in the death throes of a bad relationship. That pregnancy scare didn't help. He was my college boyfriend after the Mormon and we met and started dating when I was twenty. He was really charismatic and outspoken, he seemed smart and he was really, really tall. In addition to all that, he could dress himself competently so I pretty much thought he was perfect. As I matured a little, I realized the things you like in college (or on "asshole vacation," as I like to call it) shouldn't be the things you like as an independent, free-thinking adult with a real-life job and real-life responsibilities. Or, at least, they shouldn't be if you plan on doing any developing as a person.

At about twenty-two, I noticed that he told a lot of lies about himself to seem less boring and cowardly. He lied about people he'd been with; he lied about drugs; he lied about getting into an Ivy League school (and going there, becoming addicted to painkillers and dropping out). Moreover, I realized that he made all those racist jokes because he was actually a racist and not, I guess, the cute college kind? A polo racist? I figure you don't really understand that people can be evil in college—or that you can only know in a limited way—because it's such a contained little terrarium where everyone is entitled and depraved and self-involved. While we were in college, a lot of the things he said just made him seem provocative and unapologetic, but then two years later I had graduated and moved to the city to follow my dreams and I had an actual job, and I'm spending my Saturdays at Laundromats and fretting over bills and the stove's broken again and there's no heat until the fifth and on top of that, I'm commuting every morning with someone who'll scream, "Go back to Mexico!" at a woman whose stroller happens to be in his way and then in a terrible moment of clarity you realize it's not edgy anymore.

I graduated college in Maryland and moved to New York and really, to this guy's credit, I doubt I would have had the backbone to move to New York by myself because I was a coward, too, and that might have had something to do with our initial attraction. We found a place in Brooklyn and moved in with a mutual friend so we could split a little two-bedroom between three people. It was pretty run-down but the rent was cheap and it was on a busy street, which was important because I'm from Northern California and thus afraid of my own shadow.

I moved to New York thinking I was going to land a publishing job right away and then pretty soon I'd be going up and down escalators in Rockefeller Center wearing smart skirt suits, performing cryptic operations on my smart phone and making deals and drinking martinis at lunch and in my spare time I'd write important literary novels. Within a few years we'd land an apartment with exposed brick and exposed wooden beams and anything that could be exposed would be exposed because that's how you know you've made it and maybe I'd have a kid or something but I'd also be rich enough to have a personal trainer and private chef so the kid wouldn't ruin my body. Then I'd work from home and make a living off serious novels, while freelancing a bit in independent literary journals for the prestige. This was my two-year plan. Which is to say, the great lyric justice awaiting college students is that when reality eviscerates them, it's pretty much their own fault.

Before I knew it, I was waiting tables again, much as I'd hated doing so in college. Conveniently, I found a popular bar/restaurant near my apartment. Sadly, the owner was a coked-up psychopath who used the restaurant's large party spaces to conspicuously cheat on his very pregnant wife. The owner wasn't around so often, thankfully, but the restaurant's general manager was even more loathsome: this guy, Ian, was a repulsive toad with a heaving gut who wore tight leather vests and had a wallet chain despite being lodged somewhere in his forties. He looked like the sort of guy whose penis had a wallet chain. He was bald and so clung relentlessly to his verdant soul patch, which he cultivated with such adoration you'd think it was some kind of virility god to which he made BBQ sauce sacrifices.

Once, Ian told me without prompting about a time he went to Vegas with his girlfriend and made a few grand gambling and so procured a prostitute from one of Vegas's many prostitute stables. The telling of the story culminated with him suddenly donning a blissful faraway expression and saying of the occasion, "I didn't touch. I just enjoyed." I would have thrown up in his face were I not so perplexed by the fact he had a girlfriend. Honestly, though, self-esteem being what it is, men like this will always be able to find people who seek their validation. When I say "men like this," I mean you could smell his perineum through his jeans.

I worked and I got my ass and ego handed to me every day, as being a waiter is basically eating shit professionally. I had no real "in" to the publishing industry and my months of waiting tables in that hellish place were occasionally interrupted by applying to any job in the industry regardless of its appeal. Life was pretty bad as, I mentioned, I was too cowardly to leave a relationship that was long sour, too poor to support myself if I did, too tired and lazy when I got home from my shitty job to commit to finding a way out. Finally, months later, through a miraculous and ultimately irrelevant chain of events, I was offered an interview at a major publishing house. It was in editorial (what I wanted), however it was in the children's department. But I figured more absurd things had happened.

I was so excited and so certain that it would finally be my foot in salvation's door, my rescue from the constant sexual harassment and emotional degradation at the restaurant. I'd never have to watch the owner grope the pairs of Wild Turkey "promo sluts" (his term) in fishnets and knee-high boots and denim miniskirts who'd sit in his lap at the bar and do shots while he held their hands behind their backs and his hugely pregnant wife looked at paint swatches for the nursery in their apartment directly above. Really, the owner's tableau of coke and ego-induced self-destruction paled in comparison to being within fifty feet of Ian as he ate his nightly pulled pork sandwich, during which he spent most of the consuming part trying to extract the juice and gristle from under his permanently dirty fingernails and I swear to God the whole spectacle was so repulsive it almost made me a celibate vegetarian. Then I would go home and my unemployed live-in boyfriend would tell me how much he hated Polish people and wonder why I didn't want to sleep with him.

A lot was riding on this interview. I didn't think I had it in the bag, but I thought I had a solid chance. I put on my nicest department store skirt suit, which my mother had purchased for me in middle school, and I got on a subway to Midtown Manhattan. Before I knew it, I was looking up at the seemingly tallest building I'd ever seen and the street smelled of meat skewers and gasoline, subway vapor and aggression.

A few minutes into the interview (in which I was asked about current trends in the publishing industry and stuttered in response because I was uncertain why they expected a classics major to know anything like that, and, gosh, they didn't expect me to read books by *living* authors, did they?) the HR woman conducting the whole humiliating shitshow looked me square in the eyes, folded her hands primly and said, "I don't mean to be a dream ruiner, but..." and I kind of blocked everything out after that. I do remember she had matched her cardigan to her garish pink skirt. I also remember that look on her face: one of almost astonishing, supreme smugness. In that moment, hands folded, leaning back just so, this horrible little woman revealed herself to be more than ecstatic to dream ruin, that in fact this exact thing was her only pleasure. She meant to be a dream ruiner, and she loved it. Her features were so strung against the bones by a life of acrimony punctuated by the occasional opportunity to destroy the dreams of young morons (like myself) that her face had actually crushed into itself, giving her the appearance of such bitterness that she looked like a cat's anus in a sweater set.

I ran out of the interview and toward the subway and here I should mention that it was more than one hundred degrees and that being outside in the dead of summer in New York is like dog-paddling through a steaming hot bowl of chicken and stars and, moreover, I was wearing nylons and a cheap, ill-fitting rayon suit. I stumbled underground and onto the platform. There, waiting for a train back to my neighborhood, I began to shake and fight back the tears as I realized there was no light at the end of the tunnel, and all I had to go home to was a racist boyfriend without a job and my own job where I endured hours with my portly general manager who smelled like a corpse left out in the sun and begged me to tell him what kind of porn I watched. It was at this moment that defeat and heat exhaustion and hopelessness collapsed onto each other and I doubled over a trash can on the subway platform and threw my guts up. In front of fifty people.

As a sidenote, if you'd like to know how I've since understood the word "dehumanizing": it's throwing up in sweat-soaked rayon amid dense humidity on a packed subway platform while an impish stranger performs "Hotel California" on the pan flute for quarters and derision. To this day, I can't listen to that song. Which isn't that bad, I guess, because the Eagles are terrible. At least he didn't destroy something good.

I started back toward Brooklyn and sat there on the train suffocating in my own BO, with the taste of sour vomit in my mouth. Because I lived in a notoriously hard-to-access part of the borough, it took three trains to get anywhere. On the second train of the journey, I experienced the one and only time I have ever been verbally harassed on a subway in New York, by two boys in their early twenties who decided to discuss their plans for me should the train empty out. I listened to them tell elaborate stories of "spread[ing me] open" over the seats and how they were going to "choke" me on their cocks as I tried not to cry because I didn't want them to have the satisfaction of thinking they were the reason.

When I reached the third and final platform, waiting for the last train, I watched a baby rat teeter on the tracks either trying to walk in earnest for the first time or, perhaps more likely, ravaged by the terminal stages of rabies. It was at this point I noticed a blond girl who was also watching the baby rat. She was wearing a figure-hugging tank top and tight jeans, with all of her very alternative tattoos on display. They were mostly old-school, flair-style pinup stuff, some logos belonging to punk bands since disbanded or on major labels, some characters from cult films, some counterculture symbols like the anarchy "A" or the iron cross or the Apple logo, I don't remember which, and some dinosaurs and koi because people are boring in the same way everywhere.

I don't really remember her tattoos because I most indelibly remember her necklace: a fist-sized orb of amber, in which a scorpion had been preserved *Jurassic Park* style. She noticed me looking at her and I guess she must have noticed me looking at the baby rat, too, because she motioned to its convulsing below and said, "It's kind of cute, right?" And I nodded and forced a slight smile and looked away because I was in such a state of anxiety and panic and self-pity that if I had to even think about her faux tough-girl accessories and leather cuffs and facial piercings, I was going to throw one of us in front of the next train.

So we waited. And we waited some more. After about thirty minutes on that airless platform under stifling humidity, I found myself making eye contact with her again because I could not shake the sense that she was starting to look worse off than me. Her posture had slacked and her movements were darting.

She said in my direction, "I'm going to be late for work. I'm fucked," and I nodded again and looked away again because I had a shift at the restaurant that night, meaning my only foreseeable solace was scrubbing the taste of vomit out of my mouth. As far as I was concerned, she and her leather cuffs and Tim Burton tattoos could fuck right off because I had my own problems.

Minutes ticked on and ticked on and trains came intermittently across the station, all going in the opposite direction. On our side, people just slumped further and sweated more. I took off my jacket and looked at the baby rat for a while and thought it had so little control of its movements it was probably going to be struck by the train if the motherfucker ever pulled into the station but at least that baby rat would never resign itself to splitting the rent with a mate it used to love but now realized the mate in question genuinely believed "black people are poor out of laziness." *At least*, I thought amid the white squalls of self-pity and self-loathing, *rabies is supposed to be a really fun high before it consumes your brain and drags you to certain excruciating death, right? Like whippits?* Anything sounded better than standing there, bloated under my sweat stains in air so hot you could actually hear it hover around you.

We looked at each other again because the wait on the platform had now reached about forty-five minutes. At this point, her expression was one of total anguish. She seized on the eye contact and said, "I can't fucking believe this. I'm going to get fired for being late again. It's my third strike. I'm fucked. I'm going to lose my job. I need this fucking job."

A voice came over the loudspeakers and announced that there would be no northbound train service and it was all canceled, and the voice did not address why they couldn't have told us that forty-five minutes ago and have a nice life, suck their dicks and so forth.

Here she looked as though she were about to cry, which would have been funny in light of all her bad-girl accoutrements, but I didn't take any pleasure in it. She said, to no one in particular, "Oh my God. I'm so fucked. I don't know how to get there. I've only gotten there on the train."

I paused. I sighed and I asked, "Where do you work?"

She said the name of a restaurant about eight blocks in a straight line from my apartment and she actually did look worse off than me and—since apparently I had to walk the rest of the way too—I told her I was going that direction and she could come along with me. She thanked me profusely and we ascended the staircase into the midday sun. We walked along for a while in silence because based on our appearance— me in that sweat-soaked suit with a string of imitation pearls and her in tattoos and combat boots—our only commonality was finding the dying baby rat cute. We looked like such an odd couple that I became self-conscious and tried to make conversation. Luckily, she was pretty chatty and the moment I opened my mouth, she kind of launched into her life story.

She was from Detroit and had just moved to New York City. She was twenty-two years old and hadn't gone to college because she had a good bartending job in Detroit and figured it was better to pay rent than go into debt for a future that wasn't really guaranteed and she was kind of done with the educational system, she said, after dropping out of high school ("Like, I'm never going to actually use algebra, you know?") but she'd broken up with her live-in boyfriend after a year together and ran away to New York to become a tattoo artist or do piercings or something like that and while she was training, she'd gotten a job as a line cook at a counterculture Mexican restaurant to make ends meet. She really liked the job and boasted about how she could make an amazing seitan burrito but it was so far away from her apartment that she'd been late twice already and the joint had a draconian three-strikes policy.

Then we walked for a bit more in silence and I realized I was walking alongside a total stranger and the situation was kind of like talking to people on airplanes, insofar as regular rules of polite conversation don't really apply because you're almost certainly never going to see that person again. She was already pretty open about her life so I kind of just went

with my curiosity and said, "Why did you break up with your
boyfriend?"

"Because," she said, "he found out I did some movies before we got together."

"What do you mean?"

"Have you ever heard of—" And here she said the name of
one of those alt-porn sites along the lines of Suicide Girls that
all employ the naming convention of a modifier with negative
connotations followed by a noun with comparatively innocent
ones like Misbehaving Valedictorians or Needle Drug Mas-
seuses or Girls Who Never Had Supportive Teachers and Now
Fuck on Camera. I don't know. All the names are stupid.

I nodded.

"So I did a few scenes for them, to like, pay the rent, you
know? It was like a week of work and it's like, here's six hundred dollars, and that's a lot of money in Detroit, not like here."
She laughed and I kind of laughed too because all New Yorkers
get that joke. "And it was like, whatever, you know, it was like
me and another girl in like a dentist's office and we'd eat each
other out and then fuck this guy in the chair. It was totally
whatever, you know? Like, nothing weird. And I just did it
because it'd be like rent for a couple months for two fucking
scenes. And then I met this guy at the place where I was tend-
ing bar and we started hooking up or whatever. And, like, I
knew that he was like a really good guy because he went down
on me before I ever gave him a blowjob, you know?"

I nodded some more and was happy my eyes were completely obscured by running mascara and sweat, otherwise
they'd probably be pretty wide.

"So we hooked up a couple times and then he started coming to the bar and we'd just fuck in the bathroom while I was on shift. It was like love at first sight, you know? He was so fucking amazing. We got this place in my favorite part of Detroit, it's like the best neighborhood. And we were near my bar and this little park and it had, like, a dining room and everything. The bathroom even had one of those things that like shoot water."

"A bidet?"

"Yeah. Pretty fucking cool, right?"

It was at this point in her story that I was struck by her describing a time in her life that sounded a lot happier than mine, which I found off-putting.

"We broke up because one night we were watching porn. You ever do that? Like watch porn while you're fucking? Guys are really into it. And I was like, wanna see something really hot? So, we're like sitting at the computer and I'm in his lap, riding him, and I go to the website to show him some of my shit, you know, and it starts and he just fucking flips out and has a total shit fit. He starts screaming at me and asking about how much I've done and I told him like three or four scenes and he's like, calling me a whore and, like, a lying bitch."

At this point I think I said something like, "What an asshole!" even though the story had become so incomprehensible that I didn't really understand if this was real or if I was hallucinating from the heat. I only suspected it was real because she was talking so loudly and we were walking past this park and people with kids were looking at us.

"He walked out and when he finally talked to me again, he broke up with me and kicked me out. He didn't want to be with some whore that like, any of his friends could go online and pay twenty bucks for a membership and watch me get fucked, you know? So he fucking kicked me out. It was like he ripped my heart out and stepped all over it and I don't even understand what the big deal was because it was like a couple scenes, like a couple threesomes and some facials, you know? I mean, it's not like I was a porn star or anything. So I was like, fuck it, I'm gonna move to New York City and learn how to fucking tattoo because what do I have to lose? The love of my life just fucking kicked me to the curb for doing a couple scenes for money. When I got here, I got this necklace to re-mind me to take care of myself," and she held up the heavy chain with the preserved scorpion, "because people are like, poisonous, you know? It's like, you have to protect yourself. Some people are predators and some people just don't do that shit. So it was like, either I fucking carve it on my arm or I get the necklace."

I was nodding and looking ahead silently because this was a lot to take in. It was a weird moment for me, because I knew in a more vigilant state I would have been completely fasci-nated by her distinction between "being a porn star" and "filming a few scenes to pay the rent," as if the connotations of "porn star" are somehow more sinister than fucking a few strangers in a dentist's chair on camera. For six hundred dol-lars. It sounded like the difference between being a serial killer and one count of vehicular manslaughter eventually thrown out of court.

In fact, this distinction was so bizarre that I would have probed for further explanation had I not caught my stupid weak heart swelling up with sympathy for her. It sounded like she loved this guy and even though she mentioned nothing they had in common but sex, she and I didn't have much in common either and here I was kind of amazed by her. She had her heart broken and got dumped by someone she loved and fled everything and everyone she knew to get away from her misery. She, unlike me, actually had the backbone to pick up and leave and move to New York to pursue her dreams by herself and here she was, trying to eke it out as a line cook making alt-tacos so she could pay rent until she was done with her tattoo apprenticeship. At least in one pretty explicit way she was a lot better than me. Compared to her, I was just a coward who needed to be helped along through every significant life stage.

Then she blinked. "What about you, where are you from?" Like it was the next step in polite conversation.

I told her, "California," and it was right about then we came to my block. I pointed her in the direction of her restaurant and told her that in a few blocks, she'd start to recognize her surroundings and then she'd come to the exit of her usual subway station. It would be four blocks from there, as she knew. She thanked me with a big, weird hug and told me to come by sometime for vegan fajitas her treat and I told her I would even though I knew I wouldn't because this whole ordeal wouldn't be half as surreal if I ever saw her again. So I didn't.

It was then as I was walking down the trash-strewn street toward my apartment that I realized human suffering as it pertains to love and sex is universally awful. Sure, we came from completely different circumstances with completely different goals and frames of reference and ways of seeing the world, but at the end of the day, I was pretty heartbroken and trapped in a loveless relationship while she was pretty heartbroken having just escaped a volatile one. We were both in New York City in our early twenties, self-obsessed and pursuing stupid dreams without ever really stopping to ask why we needed to be in New York and paying New York rents to do so, but the city has a crafty way of distracting you from ever wondering that because it's too busy throwing insane situations like this exact one in your face.

I'm still kind of unclear on how the distinction between doing porn and being a porn star is more than a semantic one (maybe), but I definitely don't think you should make people who do porn feel bad about themselves. While we're at it, though, maybe don't do porn no matter how much it pays the rent because it sounds like that shit can really come back to haunt you.

So. Have some foresight. I think.

HITTING ON GIRLS IN BARS

Hitting on people is seemingly a very tricky art. We devote a lot of scenes in movies to showing characters who are good and bad at it. In all honesty, it's not very complicated: if you would like to buy a stranger a drink, don't be a skeez about it. You can either approach someone yourself or offer through the bartender. If he or she seems receptive, you should just be nice. Any person who makes someone feel like an asshole for wanting to buy him or her a drink is a bigger asshole and not worth the time. If he or she's not interested, he or she can say so like an adult. No one should ever have to feel humiliated because they want to buy someone else a drink. This is why the multimillion-dollar industry based around how to hit on people is a fragile web of lies: just be nice; don't be an asshole.

Once, when I was a teenager, a man with funny shapes shaved into his sideburns told me I was "hotter than two mice making love in a wool sock." Although this crosses no explicit lines, it is an example of something you should not do. However, it is not the extreme opposite of what you should do, that is sitting down and trying to prove your superiority to the person you're hitting on, so that his or her self-esteem gradually drains and they'll submit by fucking you.

A few months after I encountered the porn star on the subway platform, a friend of mine who'd been living in Prague visited New York. By that point, my racist boyfriend and I had parted ways. This friend happened to be a mutual friend of mine and the aforementioned racist tantrum-prone ex's, who used to boast that his WASPy name "rings of money," so we'll call him Cecil. Cecil and I decided to bury the hatchet that night and be civil so we could enjoy the company of our friend, Jack from Prague, along with another friend, Johnny, with whom we also attended college.

Despite the fragility of the situation, me, my ex-boyfriend of approximately two weeks, Jack from Prague and Johnny were all having a nice time at the bar. By "nice time," I mean I was deep in the doldrums of those critical weeks post-breakup where you would do anything to be around your recent ex, anything including but not limited to humiliating yourself and sending cryptic text messages allegedly intended for someone else. The doldrums are the point in any person's life where—should that person have any instincts toward self-preservation—he or she would do well to stay away from the ex, the point at which one is most vulnerable. By "stay away," I mean locked in your bedroom, sewed into a Onesie and wearing a helmet.

There we were, sitting outside in the back garden of our

neighborhood bar. Jack from Prague and Johnny have—for brevity's sake—an occasionally collapsed and always competitive relationship, or a tense friendship with lots of baggage. They were having a conversation about something having to do with college. I was sitting there trying to look like I wasn't utterly preoccupied with the recent breakup and what my ex was thinking and if he was as curious about me as I was about him and if this would all blow over soon and if we'd get back together and have little bigoted children together (if he didn't make me abort them!). Severing yourself from someone after several years actually corrupts the brain and one entertains such thoughts.

There I was, smoking cigarettes and slumped over and worrying about whether or not I looked pretty when, all of a sudden, a man appeared. He was tall and pasty-white, stocky if not a little doughy, with a pinched expression on a narrow head under the kind of spectacles that only a person who refers to them as "spectacles" would wear. He embodied that collision of smug condescension and social unease that you're probably familiar with if you've ever gone to a big electronics chain to get your computer fixed. Curiously, he put down a shot in front of Jack from Prague and a glass of wine in front of me. Though I'm normally not one to order wine in bars— because of pride—I was drinking wine that night, anticipating a situation I'd need to navigate unwasted.

There we were, a full drink in front of me and a shot in front of Jack from Prague. My automatic assumption in this stricken, preoccupied state was that the Stranger somehow knew Jack, had been invited to the bar by someone at this very table and the shot was a celebratory gesture, honoring Jack's return to the States from the Czech Republic. I assumed the drink for me was simply gentlemanly behavior.

Jack from Prague invited the Stranger to have a seat. It was immediately established that no one at the table had ever even seen the guy and that he was insufferable: as we raised our drinks to observe the free ones—I with my glass of wine, Jack with his shot, the Stranger with his pour of whiskey—the Stranger cautioned Jack not to breathe through his nose while swallowing, in order to somehow mask the taste of the liquor. As someone who's watched a lot of spaghetti Westerns, I knew it was dishonorable to tell a man how to drink his whiskey. Moreover, as someone who is plagued by genuine fears that the amount of whiskey in the world is finite, I knew this man was wrong.

After polite introductions around the table, the Stranger noticed that I was smoking unusual cigarettes and—much like in Denver at that awful frat party—took that as an opening to conversation by asking for one. I happily obliged because the man had just given me a full drink for no discernible reason. I offered my lighter and watched with some skepticism, as the ritual of lighting the cigarette seemed visibly foreign to him. Once it was lit, the Stranger took a few methodical puffs and then snubbed out the full cigarette. For those of you who aren't smokers, this is an astonishingly tactless move. Like punching a gift horse in the teeth.

He noticed as I watched the display with giant eyes and he said, "Too harsh."

I recoiled a little bit, but with some understanding. I have been occasionally told that the brand I smoke is harsh. I have also been occasionally told they taste like "nothing." Smokers have preferences. His display became less outrageous and more within the realm of reason (though it is still rude).

He reached into his breast pocket, with pinky finger lifted fastidiously, as if offering his shirt a spot of tea. He removed a small black box with a blue light on the side that glowed and stirred like a neon heart. From the black box, he produced a slim, plastic-looking tube.

"Now these," he said, "are really smooth."

It was at this point I realized his request for my cigarette and subsequent snubbing out had actually been a performance, a lead-in, a verse before the chorus about how objectionable he was. Not only that, I realized I had encountered my first electronic cigarette smoker, patron of a product I'd seen only in ads on the subway boasting of its value as a quitting tool (not as a cool, sexy alternative to real smoking). I could not believe my eyes as the Stranger sat there and decorously puffed away. I then wondered if I would have taken him more or less seriously had he produced a fucking bubble pipe.

Jack from Prague and Johnny resumed their conversation, perhaps trying not to call attention to this absurdity. I don't exactly recall what they were talking about but I believe Johnny was working on a paper for grad school applications and the conversation was at least loosely academic. The Stranger half-shut his eyes and mustered an extremely serious expression, as if willing his brain to assimilate the conversation and find a way to upend it. He began interjecting in a manner that indicated he saw himself as a sort of gadfly, whereas the rest of us exchanged sneaking glances to communicate puzzlement at his ornery and defensive way. My brain soon turned back on its obsession with heartbreak and loss and whether or not Cecil and I were going to end this charade and get back together.

The Stranger then turned to me with the smug, contemplative gaze of a serious man without serious thoughts and said, "Tell me, Ashley, what do you think: is there an implicit value to absolute power?"

I was visibly astounded by the question, having not heard such open, obvious pseudo-intellectualism since freshman year of college.

"What?!" I blurted.

Having not registered the look of shock on my face, he repeated himself: "I asked, is there an implicit value to absolute power." I could see in his pinched expression that he was trying to make me feel stupid by spouting transparent horseshit.

"No, no," I said, not wanting him to think he'd just blown my mind, "I heard you."

He leaned forward, gathering up his small, darting features and awaiting my admission of inadequacy. "So?"

Here I stuttered a bit, because I was more than fine with him thinking I was just staggering under awe of him and the rich thoughts within his heaving brain. Finally equipping myself to deal with the situation, I said, "That . . . that's an absurd question."

"Excuse me?"

"It doesn't mean anything."

He frowned, confused.

Here, I let the judgment play out all over my face and added, "Why would you even say that?"

Not skipping a beat, the Stranger just looked at me

squarely, yet in a flinching way, like someone who got beat up as a kid but not enough and said, "Because I enjoy going to bars and antagonizing liberal arts majors . . . and seeing if they've actually read Machiavelli."

I guess he figured that—like some god of refutation sent to watch on us and show how bad we are at speaking—he had accomplished his task. Unbeknownst to him, he'd merely confirmed he sucked, which wasn't much in doubt after he wasted one of my cigarettes like so much dry ice so that his stupid electronic ones could enter with some fanfare.

Here I decided I needed more information in order to continue. I went inside and cornered the bartender, who is a friend of mine. I wanted to know how the Stranger knew exactly what I was drinking, having spoken to none of us before sitting down.

The bartender looked very guilty and explained, "[The Stranger] came in and asked who the girl in the skull shirt was"—please note that because, developmentally, I am a twelve-year-old, I was wearing a Misfits shirt—"I said to him, 'You mean the girl who's sitting outside with her friends and her ex-boyfriend? Who she broke up with a week ago?' And [the Stranger] said, 'Yeah, what is she drinking? I'd like to buy her a drink.'" The bartender was apparently so shocked that the Stranger was not deterred by the mention of a recent ex-boyfriend at the table that he told him. Still, if the bartender's real reason was "personal amusement," I couldn't blame him. It was then I realized we were dealing with someone who had no qualms with dropping into a loaded environment and chasing tail anyway.

The bartender proceeded to explain that the Stranger had

recently become a regular of sorts and this table bombing technique had already emerged as his MO: he comes around to the bar, selects a girl, and fixates on her for the night, whether one of his comely fellow bartenders or some unsuspecting patron like myself. I'd like to note that I tend to bristle at men or women complaining of unwanted sexual attention from strangers, as it sounds like nothing more than insisting on one's appeal. My point is that I was the target this night and some poor sucker was going to be the target the next day.

Thus, the Stranger knew that one of the three men (though not *which* one) sitting outside with me was a very recent ex and, as a workaround, brought some shots and invited himself to join us. This is pretty wily but also fucking offensive.

I returned outside only to find that the Stranger had switched seats with Cecil in order to sit beside me. Considering the Stranger did not know which of these men was my recent ex, I guess asking such a thing requires a balance of balls and stupidity so volatile I admire his facility for walking without tipping over. Obviously, Cecil was entertained by the Stranger's shameless pursuit and happily obliged him. Taking my seat, I turned my chair to a suitably aggressive angle away from the Stranger and retreated into conversation with Jack from Prague.

About an hour went by and the Stranger spent the remainder of his time playing a game on his smart phone and pretending to text. He must have deduced early on that, free drinks or no, he'd made himself unwelcome, but he still just sat there. Finally, as the bartender announced that the back garden would soon close, the Stranger turned to me and said with all the urgency of someone trying to whisk me off on the Underground Railroad, "Ashley. I need to see you again."

"Why?!" I exclaimed because I was genuinely surprised. I hadn't made eye contact with him since his bit about "implicit value" and "absolute power" and adding "adjectives to nouns" so they "sound thoughtful." I thought our interacting time had reached its end and I'd thought my body language was clear enough.

He replied, "I'd like to have dinner with you and share conversation."

I'd like to interject here that I am serious. And he continued!

"Here's what you're going to do: you're going to give me your number and I'm going to call you in a few days."

Because I have a nice, puerile anti-authority streak, this is pretty much the perfect way to guarantee I will not go on a date with you. Tangentially, it's impressively gross to couch a request for a date in such domineering language.

"No," I said, "I'm not."

Furrowing his brow just a little deeper, as if simultaneously confused but more certain of himself, he said, "Yes, you are."

"What?" I had no idea what to make of this. "No."

He became fully befuddled. "Why not?"

"Now's not a good time," I said, referring to the racist elephant at the table.

"What do you mean?"

"The bartender told you," I said and looked at him with pretty open anger.

Whether or not he understood my allusion to Cecil, the

Stranger played dumb. He finished his drink in mock nonchalance—no doubt trying to avoid breathing through his nose—and got up and left.

For months after, I gave him the benefit of the doubt and assumed he was just socially awkward and trying to reconcile that with wanting to brush his goatee against my unimaginable places. Now I realize he figured—via a free drink and some blowharding about Machiavelli excerpts he'd maybe skimmed online—he might exploit the duress of my recent breakup and coerce me into a date with some pushy rhetoric no doubt nurtured on the Internet in pick-up artist forums. I wasn't receptive to this because I myself had spent tens of thousands of the government's dollars on *my* Machiavelli excerpts, which I had the decency to skim in a physical book while lazily highlighting passages I would never remember.

Again, you should never be nasty and ungrateful about someone wanting to talk to you because he or she finds you attractive. It takes a lot of courage to approach a stranger. However, I am going to take offense to anyone propositioning me with "Here's what you're going to do . . ." and also, "You're probably not that smart and I like antagonizing you because of that." For the record, if I were horrible enough to be sexually aroused by men who like to think they read books but kind of just look at the words, New York would make me so full of babies I'd have to shoehorn them out to make room for my organs.

The Stranger has since furthered his reputation for being an aggressive sleaze and ambushing girls at the bar with his electronic cigarettes and button-down shirts tucked into jeans. A friend of mine saw him recently strolling along in North Brooklyn with one such lucky lady on whom, apparently, his method worked. The Stranger was wearing a crisp new shirt emblazoned with the logo of a jam band and puffing away on his beloved electronic cigarettes.

Hearing that, I experienced a single piercing moment in which I imagined us together, discussing Machievelli and speed-reading Nietzsche and laughing, just laughing, because who needs thoughts when you can have opinions? And then we'd have middling, stilted sex and we'd smoke electronic cigarettes in the shadows after and then I realized my recent breakup had impossibly colored my perception of "settling" and that dying is really just more noble.

SEXUAL FANTASIES

People always tell me I have a "rich inner life." I used to be pretty flattered by that until I realized, after a few years, it just meant "I think you have Asperger's." In reality, I do not have a rich inner life. For one thing, I don't masturbate. I guess it all started when I was a teenager and didn't masturbate.

It's important to note that I'm not trying to portray myself as some sort of person free of sexual impulse and full of virtue. In a lot of ways, it was just a by-product of confusion—I didn't know what I was supposed to do, if it was inside stuff or around stuff, if I'm supposed to brush my teeth before (or after)—but I obviously don't think masturbation is bad. For example, I think people who try to punish kids for masturbating are insane, imposing no small amount of guilt on their children unnecessarily and also stupid because trying to keep kids from masturbating is like trying to play Whac-A-Mole with your hands tied behind your back. Which is not to suggest you should try to stop kids from masturbating by using your teeth. That's dark.

My objection to masturbation is purely personal: I cannot bring myself to do it. I consider this more of a hang-up than any indication of valor. In moments of drunken vulnerability, I have admitted as much to close friends. These people always look at me like I'm crazy to think they'd ever be interested in the state and welfare of my vagina. I'm glad when I can discern this particular look of pained disinterest because some grasp of nonverbal communication indicates that—though I certainly fall somewhere on the autism spectrum—I'm probably not full-blown.

Basically, I tried. I tried occasionally as a teenager. I always knew that I was different and off and something was probably wrong with me because I didn't masturbate, so—because peer pressure is such that one can buckle to it even when alone—I gave it a few shots. Sadly, no matter how much I tried, it never worked out. The problem, so far as I can distinguish it, is that I just can't shake the suspicion the act itself looks so pathetic. Consequently, I tell myself I do not masturbate because I am too cerebral and, because in order to be a good liar one must lie to oneself first, I do all right. As a sidenote, can you imagine what kind of hero you'd have to be to look noble while jerking off? If anyone can do it, I'd guess a fireman. But even then, I'm skeptical.

I always knew this lack of a normal teenage habit was strange. I recall getting a lecture from a friend in college who told me I'd be doomed to a lifetime of terrible sex if I didn't know how to please myself. I recall that statement smarting at the time because it sounded so reasonable but I could never convince my brain that a human being hunched over and gravely trying to pleasure itself is anything but the most concise expression of sadness I can fathom, excepting maybe "dead puppy on the floor of an abandoned toy store."

Herein exists something fascinating to me: it seems safe to conclude that in order to get around any recognition of how small and sad one looks while masturbating, those who masturbate—that is, the many—require muscular imaginations. It's impressive enough that, with some physical prodding, the imagination can actually create sexual gratification out of nothing. Going further, the imagination not only forges and sustains arousal, it can actually overcome the nagging certainty we all must experience that we look completely ridiculous while doing so. The imagination performs a ballet around your hunched back, gritted teeth and desperate machinations.

The acumen required to compartmentalize and set aside just how pathetic one looks while trying to get oneself off leads me to believe that everyone who masturbates is either terminally ignorant or a genius. Masturbation is not the listless rustle of a pedestrian mind, it would seem, but the activity of kinetically imaginative ones.

This is fascinating because ideas aren't just doled out freely to anyone. As someone who works in a field that requires its labor force to, essentially, generate ideas all day long, I can confirm that it's challenging (I don't binge drink because I'm not creative). Tangentially, I really can't say enough of alcohol, which takes ordinary moments and impregnates them with startling magic, like Russian literature and inhalants. My point is simply that I have what I figure to be an above-average if not occasionally robust imagination and yet, apparently, not one as robust as those who masturbate, which is to say every other human, including ones without limbs.

It would appear that regular people do have rich inner lives and, trust me—trends in overdiagnosis to the contrary—the entire world does not have a developmental disorder. If it did, life would involve much less eye contact and much more off-putting non sequiturs, spontaneous crying and pronouncements of how quickly you can drink an entire Dr Pepper in one gulp. (Eleven seconds.) Also, wearing costumes would become more socially acceptable for adults.

When I use that expression, "rich inner life," I don't mean it in the sense of trying to sugarcoat these supposed learning disabilities, social anxiety or other stymied development. What I mean is that people—normal, shitty people, the kind you see everywhere, clogging streets and subways with their sagging guts and coughs and half-formed ideas and nonexistent attention spans and their *fucking hats*—have exceedingly rich inner lives. They must, you see, because they can bring themselves to orgasm. I jerk off ergo sum.*

Let's pause a moment and define our terms. When I am astounded by people's ability to masturbate, I mean without the aid of pornography. That's really important. If you're masturbating to porn, you're not doing anything impressive to anyone. There is nothing magnificent about ejaculating on

---

* ("Cogito ergo cum" seemed too precious.)

yourself while watching some guy with a goatee choke out a twenty-five-year-old dressed as a sixteen-year-old.

More to the point, when I talk about the role of imagination in masturbation, what I'm really describing is sexual fantasy. I'm referring to those intimate narratives, those cinematic movements we pull from the ether of ourselves, to distract us from whatever it is we're doing long enough to cull an orgasm from our genitals.

Perhaps largely due to its foreignness, I am profoundly impressed by spontaneous masturbation. For example, a friend of mine—we'll call him Percy Shelley, thanks to his romantic disposition—was once a teenager and housesitting for a neighbor. I guess "housesitting" isn't the most accurate term; he was really being paid peanuts to maneuver through the neighbor's garage and feed their cat a few times while they were out of town. One day, Percy was standing in the neighbor's garage and decided, for no apparent reason, that he was going to masturbate right then and there. His second thought was much more reasonable: he should, in fact, not masturbate in his neighbor's garage. Surely that was illegal, somewhere. Then, because outrage is the only sensation that subsumes fear in teenagers, he had a third thought: his distaste for the patriarch of the household, a humorless police officer who lectured him frequently, and it was at that moment, pressed between a Volvo and the stairwell to the house, Percy undid his pants.

More remarkable still, just as he was nearing climax, the family cat—the very being whose care had been entrusted to Percy—appeared through the cat door. It scurried over, having already come to associate him with food. The cat began to purr and weave at Percy's ankles, wrapping its tail around his shins. All the while, Percy was still able to masturbate. When he climaxed, intending to hit the greasy, oil-slicked garage floor, he ended up getting a little on the cat. He then filled the food dish and went home.

I find this spectacular. How can you have an orgasm in a cold, empty garage while a cat tries to manipulate you with affection? At what point do you ignore the little voice that says, *This is pretty weird*, and just keep on trucking? That is where I identify the role of imagination.

Some of you may be horrified by this. I'm not because I'm a dog person, but I understand why people recoil when I explain my friend ejaculated on someone else's cat. I guess it doesn't really matter *whose* cat it was, so they may just be horrified he ejaculated on anyone's cat. Still, it's not all that terrible because it's not like he did something that made the cat so uncomfortable it would have to go through years of therapy. The cat probably forgot it had semen in its fur two seconds later, if it even noticed at all. Obviously, if Percy had somehow forced the cat to masturbate him, then it would be a different situation because it would be animal abuse and the cat would absolutely have to go to therapy and address its trauma in a direct way. My point is that Percy didn't do anything wrong, so let's set aside our judgment and just admire his ability to achieve orgasm in hostile conditions.

This brings me to what I consider the most spellbinding testament to the capacity of human imagination: masturbating at work. Yes, the workplace. The least thrilling and most oppressive arena of day-to-day life. The phenomenon of the discreet work jerk-off is about as awe-inspiring as the aurora borealis, Keith Richards and time-lapse footage of flowers growing: they all fall under the banner of miracles.

I don't know about you, but I have worked many shitty desk jobs in which I go into the office at nine a.m., rotely answer forty emails of varying inconsequence, plug data into multiple templates no one will ever look at, highlight dubiously relevant information in a one-hundred-and-fifty-page document no one will ever read, chew a bag lunch at my desk in a joyless bovine way, get yelled at for doing my job with suspicious competence and then spend an hour mailing things to people they may never look at. All the while I know that, at the end of the day, I'll stare down a forty-minute commute in a suffocating underground metal tube pressed against a stranger who hasn't showered seemingly in weeks only to arrive at a squalid hellhole where I will continue gaining weight as I try to better obscure my bachelor's degree because no matter where I hide it, I can always sense it looming, judging me. Five days a week of this—frankly a very ordinary kind of crushing entry-level job one is lucky to obtain upon graduating college with a nonsense degree—and it's a wonder that people can still achieve any kind of sexual pleasure at all, much less provide it for themselves.

And yet . . . yet! Some people manage to enjoy orgasms in the middle of this mind-numbing day. Regular people everywhere can apparently set aside their unrelenting pressures and stress and deadlines and answering those emails with mounting anxiety between the unending ring of phones and the sputter of an always-broken copy machine and they can just duck into the restroom and masturbate, like withdrawing money from an ATM if such a transaction occurred in a cramped toilet stall under urgent silence and was extremely dehumanizing. I know this happens because I have spoken to many friends who are more than willing to admit that the lunch-hour jerk-off can sometimes be the difference between a bad day at work and a better one. Granted, you may be thinking, *I'd doubt the integrity of your poll, Ashley, it sounds like your friends are compulsive masturbators.* Selection bias is an insidious thing.

I understand if you work in some job where you make millions a year, something like finance, and you get a private bathroom, in which case I don't think masturbating at work indicates a stalwartness of character. After all, you don't have to crush other people with your sadness if they need to use the next stall over because, generally speaking, jobs in finance afford lavish private bathrooms with marble floors and gold fixtures and I've even heard they all come with an eighteen-years-and-a-day-old Brazilian girl who quietly sucks you off when you're done peeing and you never see her again because she gets replaced with another girl a day younger like so many bath tissues with breasts that point heavenward. Which is weird for the record, Wall Street, and exactly this kind of conspicuous consumption that makes regular folks derisive of your station. We have to worry about our jobs.

If you're a normal shitty person like me, however, and your office restroom isn't padded with hot, sexual favor–giving ESL teenagers, you have to rely on your own shitty imagination and force of will. Which is our focus anyway, masturbation requiring fairly lucid access to the creative faculties. Orgasm achieved through nothing but the imagination.

I guess what I'm trying to say is that masturbating at work is proof of God. Or, at least, compelling evidence of a higher power.

You'll recall I don't believe in God because they didn't get me early enough, but if they had somehow managed to sit me down as a child and explain that people everywhere can overcome the horrifying banalities of their existence and masturbate with efficacy, I might have opened my heart to Jesus or one of his colleagues. The fact that people can actually fight back against those banalities and check out for fifteen minutes from their oppressive desk jobs and go masturbate under fluorescent lights in a beige bathroom stall while staring at generations of stupid graffiti is phenomenal. It's so phenomenal that I'm practically shocked I've never read about it in the two-page portion of celebrity weeklies allotted to human interest stories, where you always hear about babies surviving hurricanes or some guy who gets disfigured in a tractor accident and everyone in his small town pools their money for reconstructive surgery and then he's still kind of a mutant so the photographer has to shoot from only one side but none of the townspeople feel ripped off because they're compassionate. What I'm trying to say is that a much more truthful—and, frankly, inspiring—story in those pages would be BELEAGUERED EDITORIAL ASSISTANT MAKING $27K A YEAR IN NEW YORK CITY WITH STUDENT LOANS MANAGES TO ACHIEVE ORGASM ALONE IN PUTRID OFFICE BATHROOM STALL. I'd read that; I wouldn't just skip it and keep reading about fictional diets attributed to famous people.

Although it's certainly not as impressive in men. For males of the species, sexual fantasy and creative stimulation are simple: first you imagine having a dick so big you have to wrap it around your thigh in order to walk and then, like clockwork, you have an erection. Once men have an erection, climaxing is all but guaranteed (right?) because all sexual fantasies for (straight) men can be reduced to a single idealized image: a marine biologist lingerie model with wings.

I'll unpack that briefly: the ideal woman is a marine biologist lingerie model with wings. First, she's a marine biologist because straight men don't actively want stupid women *but* they also don't want a woman who's so smart that she might win an argument or have cooler records or better taste in something. Therefore, the ideal woman's occupation falls in the soft sciences, like marine biology, which is essentially just looking at whales and shit. Next, she's a lingerie model because her breasts and stomach need to look perfect regardless of the manner in which you're degrading her, which can be complicated because we've already established the vivacity of your fucked-up head. Last, the ideal woman has wings. Obviously, invisible wings, because wings you can see is just weird.

Once men with erections have even partially envisioned this ideal woman, they can just climax (the actual masturbating part comes mostly from a sense of obligation). Once they've ejaculated, they become crushed by self-loathing, which means their imaginations are also remarkable insofar as they must always overcome the certainty they will hate themselves after. But they do and they keep masturbating, because men are survivors.

All of this is downright desultory compared to the ability of the fairer sex. Men don't concern themselves with details when compared to their counterparts. In case you didn't know, women's sexual fantasies are an infinite cosmos of appalling.

This is where things become weird to the point of terror. When I originally took to the Internet in a pseudo-scientific effort to understand what people think about when they masturbate, I almost couldn't believe the twisted portrait of women that emerged. Do me a favor: next time you're at a coffee shop and you notice a normal-looking woman in line behind you, wearing her unflattering pleated pants, with her long stringy hair and plain face, you need to stop thinking she's nice and come to terms with the fact that her brain is fucking crazy. See the woman walking past you on the side-walk, with her little dog in its little sweater, and her orthope-dic shoes? You wouldn't believe the putrid shit tapestries she has to weave in order to make herself come. Look at her.

It was amid this learning about sexual fantasies that I realized why I didn't masturbate: women who masturbate are all pathologically insane. This isn't some Victorian-era "hys-teria" misogyny here, it's true: the only way women get off is by imagining themselves into incredibly sophisticated narra-tives that make absolutely no sense. At least curvaceous arch-angels who love dolphins have a pretty universal appeal. Women, on the other hand, fantasize seemingly as an act of madness.

Here are some real sexual fantasies—culled from friends, lady magazines, and obscure Internet erotica—had by regu-lar women, the kind of women you see every day. This list is what I affectionately call Eight Basic Plots for Female Masturbation:

1. Trapped in haunted mansion during Samhain, the Gaelic harvest festival. Thunderstorms rage beyond. Must have revelatory but tender oral sex with every member of an all-male a capella group in separate rooms . . . unbeknownst to each other.

2. Saved from getting mugged in alleyway by ruggedly handsome, mysterious stranger. Turns out he's telekinetic with metal bones and intense, preternatural passion.

3. An emotionally complicated, brooding vampire has to kidnap me and rape me repeatedly. Not because he wants to . . . because he's been ordered to by his coven. But he can't help falling in love along the way.

4. I'm friends with a bunch of famous guys and fuck them a lot.

5. I'm a cool runaway with ruffian glamour and just met a handsome con man with a mischievous smile. Even though he's a bad boy, he's tamed by his feelings and we break into an abandoned asylum to have hungry marathon sex. Then he dies tragically trying to save me.

6. A misunderstood mutant and I find solace in each other. I'm an Olympic medalist who can see the future (but not overmuscled). He has a six-foot projectile tongue and a cock like a bear.

7. Rescued from a speeding stagecoach by darkly handsome outlaw on horseback. He

takes me back to his makeshift camp. He
dresses my wounds while undressing me.
Then we must bathe.

8. I'm a thinner version of myself and clothes
look great on me.

Holy shit, right? Every fantasy had by a single woman is
some variation on one of these eight basic plots. It's important to note "single" woman because the second women start
getting sex on the reg, their clitorises retract into their abdomens and then orgasms are boring and they have headaches
and feel bloated and didn't shave their butts that morning and
I'd rather eat this waxy American candy bar and recognize
the dull alienation I feel from my own body as a poignant
metaphor for the alienation that distances me more each day
from the man I used to love. Do you want to just order Thai?

Maybe you don't believe it. I barely do. This all seems so
elaborate that I don't know how anyone could just lie back in
the shower and close her eyes and then "God I've missed you,
Grimly Resigned to Rape Me Vampire!!" and just come. But it
happens every day. It's happening everywhere right now, all
around you. Which takes us back to my initial hang-up: that
pleasuring oneself is absurd and deeply sad and no amount of
elaborate storytelling is going to distract me from that, therefore I am incapable of something almost everyone else in the
world can do and for that I blame my failed imagination. At
least you can rest assured that everything I've written here is
factual and true—after all, how could I make any of this up if
my imagination is so atrophied?—and further, I am completely trustworthy.

As a happy ending, never masturbating has made me pretty frustrated and uncomfortable all the time, but it's also enabled me to pursue countless creative endeavors like obsessive list making, alphabetization of seemingly unrelated ideas and scrawling frenzied Latin over every visible surface of my apartment in my own blood. This is why I'm a pretty firm believer that kids should watch six hours of television a day from infancy to stymie the imagination as much as possible and then no one will masturbate ever and be just as productive as me and not irrationally angry all the time. I'm betting.

Until that happens, and we all float through our day-to-day existence as listless automatons that never climax, I do find solace in the human race and its ease with and love of masturbating (even at work). It really does demonstrate the influence of a higher power or intelligence. That's something you should contemplate whenever you relieve yourself at the office. Next time you do so, just know there may be a wad of rich inner life geysering into a handful of toilet paper right beside you. But don't be grossed out, because it simply means there is God *all around us.*

SEX, LIES AND PUBIC HAIR

As a teenager, I used to tell people I didn't have any body hair below my collarbone. Those people would always look me in the eye and waves of realization would wash over them as they quietly sussed out I was basically volunteering—in a manner I considered quite titillating then—that I had no pubic hair. This was a half-truth for a couple reasons.

Well, mostly, this demonstrates the fundamental shittiness of teenagers: they will say and do anything for attention (even bad attention). Most of the things you say to people as a teen are just horseshit self-mythology and, especially, the kind of self-mythology that's supposed to make you seem more desirable. In retrospect, it's pretty gross that I would ever say in casual conversation, "I have no body hair (*You know what that means, right?*)," but really I was just trying to seem more alluring, because if porn has taught us anything it's that vulvas should look like newborn whales without eyelashes. Which is weird, because the consequence of that is some people like vaginas to look like whatever's going to crown out of them after the copulating has taken place and that's kind of a round-about way to express a mating impulse.

Yes, some men want to penetrate vaginas that look like things coming out of vaginas (the startling conclusion is babies) or at least that's what Internet alarmists say to each other in comment threads amid all the other outrages. That, and adult films are turning all men who watch them into child molesters, I guess because pedophilia is no longer a psychiatric disorder and instead just what happens when you watch a lot of big-budget porn and pretty soon all people will expect women to shave away their pubic hair and wear plastic shoes and all men will speak in lecherous, stilted monotone and get barbwire tattoos. It doesn't seem like girls are grossed out by male pubic hair, which I guess is because porn tells us it's fine for men to have a rotten sprout salad down there or because girls never watch porn, ever, and if they did they'd probably be chi-mos, too.

I learned a lot about sex from the Internet and people on there have some harsh words for pubic hair. Apparently it's disgusting. I guess a lot of the Internet is composed of fourteen-year-old boys giggling at themselves over witticisms like, "I don't want hair in my food," and in their defense, they've never been near a naked woman and they're so high right now. I imagine if anyone supplying a lot of that anti-pube rhetoric were to come in contact with a naked woman he'd probably stroke her body hair lovingly even if it looked like algae. I get it, though, because I find the Internet pretty terrible unless I'm high, too.

Which brings me to the main point here: no one should care this much about pubic hair. No one. Sure, you can have a preference, if you really need one, but if you're the sort of person who gets into bed with someone and is upset by his or her pubic hair, you have entered the realm of being a ridiculous asshole.

Surprisingly, this extends to just about every seemingly polarizing aspect of the female body that is so widely debated on the Internet. A quick perusal of comment threads will reveal that no matter how lean, toned and glowing with health a woman appears, there's going to be a dozen opposing views on how she looks: "She's fat," "She's a bag of bones," "Her hips are too wide," ". . . Too narrow," "She's overmuscled," "Knock-kneed," "Is that a happy trail?" and such.

It's important to remind yourself that these are the opinions of virgins. Anyone who cares that much about the specifics of a person's body suffers from a kind of putrefaction of the brain, which can sometimes be caused by puberty but also by a litany of other factors: insecurity, want of attention and (of course) hating yourself.

I started eradicating all body hair around age fifteen, several years before I became sexually active. It happened one day after a friend and I were walking around the mall looking for punk rock shirts and she casually mentioned that she was itchy because she hadn't shaved in a few days.

Startled, I asked what she meant.

"I haven't shaved down there," and she used her arm like a windshield wiper across her lower body, standing beneath a display of replica tour shirts from the seventies made in 2001.

"You shave that?"

She gasped. "You don't?"

"... No. Why would I?"

"Because it makes sex way better."

It seemed legit.

Here's a nice summary of what I knew about sex at this point in my life: if one engages in anal sex, one risks the possibility of shitting out one's vagina. Sounds awful, right? When I was fifteen, I heard countless lies and untruths and blatant fabrications about sex that I took for gospel until I actually started having it, the act of which became a years-long project of systematically undoing all those stupid preconceptions, among them one described by a friend in high school named Alison, who gravely intoned that if you have anal sex too many times, you could end up "shitting out your vagina." Seriously. No high school girl should ever have to try to sleep at night haunted by the idea that if she lets a guy put it in her ass x number of times, the abrasiveness of his penis (a legendarily abrasive instrument) against her anus could actually tear the delicate, lacelike fabric of skin separating the anus from the vaginal cavity and cause her to shit out her vagina and how curious are you to find out the value of x? But wait, how did Alison know? Because she knew of course, like all the girls knew, that disgraced popular girl Lacey Norman had let football captain Mark Schuster put it in her ass a lot and, now, when she's in the restroom everyone can hear all the centimeters traveled as Lacey Norman heaves a gutful of excrement out her twat.

The idea that removing one's pubic hair makes sex better is *preposterous*. But, peer pressure being what it is, I set about trying to be a little more like my comparatively womanly friends. It continued on as part of my daily routine until my midtwenties, about the time when you (hopefully) realize that if you aren't doing it for yourself, you shouldn't be doing it.

Moreover, I began thinking about all kinds of exciting things I could do with pubic hair and all the intricate ways in which I could ornament it. I could get it those little dinosaurs and palm trees that people use to decorate twenty-five-dollar ice cream cakes and then maybe, just maybe, I'd construct one of those vinegar volcanos you see in middle school science fairs and put that down there, too. Then I'd learn to play the *Jurassic Park* theme on the piano but I'd play it very slow (in a moving way) so when the volcano erupts, it would represent something and be poignant.

I also thought a lot about how I'd style it (around the dinosaurs and vinegar flows). I'd probably shave a lot of funny messages in there, like "This Makes You Gay" just to fuck with people. Or I'd stencil a cool drawing of your parents. Or I'd braid a tiny battery-powered lightbulb into it so my vagina would look like one of those menacing deep-sea fish with the light in front of its mouth. Then penises would be like little helpless minnows swimming toward a grisly death. I really liked animals growing up, so it would also be a cool nod to my childhood. Even better, I could get pants and cut the crotches out and then make it look like my pubic hair was wearing little costumes. I see people with their dumb teacup dogs in sweaters all the time, and that strikes me as way less dignified than trying to do something nice for your body and feel pretty. Also, my vagina could fend for itself if left to its own devices way longer than a puggle.

What's weird about all this is that sometime ago pubic

hair became a political statement. It's become a challenge to make decisions about your own maintenance without those decisions being influenced by a larger cultural pressure one way or another. If a woman shaves her pubic hair, it's like she's a passive bystander injected with the sexist notion that the vagina is a cool sex hole and not part of the female reproductive system. But if she has pubic hair, she loves jam bands (which is worse than no one wanting to fuck you).

I found no compelling reason to excise pubic hair other than (1) it grosses fourteen-year-old boys out and (2) laser treatment might be what it sounds like. Seeing as how I don't plan to have sex with teenage boys ever (unless they could love me) and scientists probably don't let you play laser tag for hours until it all wilts off and never grows back because your follicles are so thrilled they all dislodge in unison, I'm not sold. Beyond that, I don't know why anyone would opt out of having pubic hair if they weren't personally bothered by it.

What all of this boils down to is that if anyone ever expresses such a strong preference for pubic hair or no, for thin or no, for muscular or otherwise, it's best not to fuck that person. In fact, that person needs to stop fucking people entirely and go read a book, maybe spend a few months in silence and consider why they are such a weird, fetishistic asshole. If you sleep with people based on their fitness as regards to a mental checklist involving disembodied parts and how they should look, you're probably way too young to be having sex.

Extreme aesthetic preference gets in the way of actually having sex. In order for sex to be good, one needs to discard reservations about one's thinness or the size of one's cock or what angles are the most flattering or how one's breasts look in whatever position because those distinctions matter only to the wrong people. The human race would also do well to let go of the idea that sex should be sanitary and dramatic and paced like a movie, because movie sex is a lie. Unless, of course, you want ponderous, candlelit missionary forever. In which case, shave everywhere but your head and start dieting and practicing your fake orgasms, because there is no hope for you. It's quite like anything in life, really: if you're that concerned with how it looks, it's going to be shallow. Or worse: boring.

Sadly, though, the pubic hair political battle will never be waged on the swath of flesh between my legs I like to call Antietam. All the years of shaving have caused, I guess, my pores to atrophy or something. All I can grow down there is a single hair. It's long and lonely and thin and scraggly. Like a coke nail. Every time I see it, I kind of feel like it's a wounded soldier left behind on the battlefield, but I guess you have to count your blessings.

INFIDELITY

I'm inclined to think that the very worst aspects of human character come out with respect to sexuality. Once, I was talking to a friend in a bar and explaining to him what sorts of perversions I thought were the most abhorrent in humanity; child molestation and rape were pretty high up there. He listened for a while and paused in a very serious way because he's read a lot of Nietzsche and then he said that human sexuality exists outside the bounds of morality. I thought about that for a few minutes and concluded he was wrong. I guess it was kind of misleading to begin with this anecdote because I'm not going to explore it any further.

Without morality, people would just be running around pissing on each other and having sex with inanimate objects. Granted, neither of those things have any real repercussions and so long as they're performed between consenting adults, I see no problems with them really but I have to find a way to end this sentence and save face. So we impose a system of basic morals on human sexuality because human sexuality is occasionally inclined to darkness. If you don't believe me, Google any word you can imagine after the phrase "jammed full of."

If we want autonomy over our sex lives and want to traverse our desires without shame and humiliation, then we should also ask of ourselves some ethics. There are a few basic rules that most of us already abide by—don't fuck children; don't rape people; don't fuck animals—but there are also ones less adhered to that are equally important: don't have unprotected sex with strangers if you know you have an STD; don't use sex to manipulate or hurt people. In short, don't be an asshole.

We run into this a lot with cheating. Infidelity is the space in which people are often capable of completely repugnant behavior and will find obtuse justification for that behavior. Or no justification at all. Which is more terrifying.

Before anyone insists "My lover loves that I have lovers!" by "cheating" I don't mean open relationships, swinging or just a general rejection of monogamy (also, alliteration is annoying). Infidelity cannot exist between consenting adults because the person being cheated on can't, by design, give consent.

I had a coworker once who was a well-educated cosmopolitan woman with an impressive bust-to-waist ratio. She was also a mentally unstable wreck who collected empty cigarette packs, even though she didn't smoke. Not that collecting empty cigarette packs would make sense if you were a smoker.

It's not like there are cigarettes in there. Once, she trapped me in my office to tell me about the middle-aged Russian man she met at a smoothie bar and with whom she had sex later that night, which led to a shouting match, which led to him running from her apartment semi-naked. And she didn't understand why he hadn't called the next day. Also, he had bizarre symbols tattooed on the shaft of his penis. So I guess she didn't understand a couple of things.

Even though she'd often confide in me about her personal life, she'd go get drunk with other coworkers and tell them she thought I was a cunt and how I had a huge potbelly but also that she thought I had an eating disorder. Which confused me in light of the confiding she'd do, but I'm not some behavioral scientist qualified to talk about complex social constructs (I'm just writing about human sexuality). Further, if you think someone has an eating disorder, you probably want to avoid humiliation hinging on his or her potbelly. Further still, I do not take kindly to people badmouthing Ajax.

The reason I'm telling you about this person, Maude, is that one time she slipped into work about an hour late and looked like she'd had a long night. She came into my office and shut the door quietly and announced that she'd been making some very bad decisions lately and had decided to stop. Without any solicitation from me, she revealed she'd been fucking one of our male coworkers. They'd run into each other at a bar some weeks ago, got wasted and went back to her place. This had happened a couple times since.

She was looking a bit worse for the wear that morning because our male coworker had ended things the night before. I guess when she said *she'd* decided to stop making bad deci-

226 | ASHLEY CARDIFF

sions, what she meant was she hadn't decided anything and in fact the outcome had been decided for her. She really shouldn't have presented it that way. She then laid into him for being selfish and leading her on.

As she was talking, my face got kind of scrunched up and incredulous and I said, "Doesn't he have a serious girlfriend?" which explains why my expression was so incredulous.

She nodded.

"Doesn't he . . . live with her?"

She nodded some more.

"Doesn't that . . . seem relevant?"

Here she shrugged and said, "That's between him and his girlfriend."

This was one of the most unnerving, inhumane things I have ever witnessed. It is right up there with the first time I learned about the concept of murder, the Ebola virus and also riding in the sky buckets at Disneyland. Thank God they got rid of those. *Who were they even for?*

Maude had just admitted to being a willing accomplice in our coworker's act of infidelity. Moreover, she was remorseless to the point of befuddlement at my questioning. This, in turn, befuddled me because I did not understand why I had not yet pegged her for a sociopath, considering every single one of her behaviors. I think the term "sociopath" gets thrown around when people don't really understand the implications. Even though it's actually a serious personality disorder, people will employ the term just to endow their informal observations of human behavior with a certain faux medical expertise. *People like me.*

"Doesn't that bother you?" I asked.

"Why would it?"

At this point, I was starting to actually question if I was the crazy one. "Well . . ." I trailed off, "he has a girlfriend." Figured I should give that another shot.

"It's none of my business," she replied, "I'm not forcing him to cheat on her."

"No, but . . ."

"If he wants to mess around with someone, he's a grown man and can make that decision himself."

"Right, but . . ."

She shrugged, a big, affected, disingenuous shrug meant to display how much time she hadn't spent even bothering to consider this. "I don't think he'd cheat on her if he was happy."

"I'm not disagreeing with that. At all. But doesn't it bother you that you're the one he's cheating with?"

She shrugged again, with an almost breathtaking indifference and said, "All's fair in love and war."

I love a platitude as much as the next guy. If I had a car it would be covered in bumper stickers. Funny ones, mostly, but definitely some about religion and politics. However, this particular platitude is loathsome. For example, there are such things as *war crimes*. Which we prosecute. People who say "all's fair in love and war" are not familiar with the Geneva Conventions. Appropriating that prosaic bit of nonsense to callously justify fucking around with someone who's involved just makes it sound like your high school history class skipped the Nuremberg trials.

"Well," I said, "can you agree that if you were in her position and you found out your live-in boyfriend was sleeping with a coworker, you'd be upset?"

"Yeah, but I'm not her."

I nodded because I, too, recognized the distinction.

She went on: "I mean, she must not be making him happy . . ." And here she trailed off and wore a flat expression as if to imply that their sex life was unsatisfying to him, thus driving him to cheat with her: Maude, Poseidon of the Boudoir.

I told her I didn't think it was possible for her to make that call, from her position, but I was beginning to realize she just didn't understand the point I was trying to make.

"Look, I don't know. Maybe she's let herself go or something."

"Um, okay." I decided to take a few steps back. "Can you at least agree that cheating is a bad thing? And that's probably why it's synonymous with deceit?" After all, that's why we call it "cheating," and not "making babies smile" or "feeding artisanal bread to ducks."

She nodded a little bit this time.

"So you can agree that cheating is bad and not, say, for example, good?" Socrates would be proud.

"I'm not his girlfriend and he's a grown-up. What he does is on him."

"Look, clearly what he's doing sucks—"

She scowled.

"What I don't understand is how you can recognize that and admit that it sucks but not see yourself as participating in it."

"Fine," she said and her nostrils flared, "is that what you want? You want me to admit that I'm doing something bad? Fine. But why not blame him? He's the one who's actually cheating on his girlfriend."

"Well . . . but you're both doing something wrong."

"You know what? I don't even know why the fuck I came in here. So you could judge me? I was being honest with you. It took a lot to come in here and admit that."

Admit what, exactly, I don't think she was sure, considering her refusal to acknowledge any wrongdoing and also claiming she'd put a stop to something that had been stopped for her. The "I was being honest" defense is always the last refuge of shitty people.

She stood abruptly and added, "I put myself out there and you just knocked me down to feel better about yourself," before storming out of my office.

It was in that moment something pretty critical dawned on me: if she were a sociopath, *she'd be nicer.* She'd also probably be smarter, because it's my understanding that sociopaths are gregarious and enterprising and can convince you of things and other stuff I'd probably know if I wasn't intellectually lazy and attempted to understand my accusations before making them.

This was all very important because it led to my second realization: if my coworker was not a sociopath, she might actually be normal. Her bizarre line of reasoning and refusal to identify any kind of culpability of her own might be a common human thing. That because she enjoyed having sex with our coworker, she was going to continue to do so. She knew full well that he had a girlfriend he'd been living with for a few years and did it anyway. It was like she was on some kind of Seesaw of Immorality, with his girlfriend on the Sucker's Side and her on the fun No-Accountability Orgasm Side, which is basically what *The Art of War* is about.

Of course, for the one being cheated on, it's a lot more complicated than that.

It happened a little over a year into living in New York. Cecil had been distant since we moved to the city. I didn't think much of it because he'd also been depressed: he hated his succession of temp jobs, hated that he had to work for the year before law school, which he especially hated because the school—due to his unremarkable LSAT performance—was third tier. Still, despite his gathering bigotry and other grating personality traits that began to reveal themselves post-college, I had at least pegged him for a loyal person.

One night, he left his phone on my desk and I noticed an undeniably suggestive text flash across the screen. The sender had a girl's name, one he'd never mentioned. I picked up his phone and read through an extensive back-and-forth between him and a woman named Leah, a coworker, I learned, who wanted to know his email address so she could send him pictures of her sexy Halloween costume. She had gone as Liza Minnelli's burlesque performer from *Caberet* and was "sad" she hadn't gotten to "show it to [him]." He replied by giving her an email address I didn't know he had.

I called him into our bedroom and asked him if he had any email addresses I didn't know about. I wanted to see the extent of his untruth. He told me he didn't and looked at me like I was crazy. I told him I knew he was lying. He stuttered, affecting sudden clarity, and told me he kept another account for his online poker persona. I told him he was going to open the account in front of me.

This was one of the strangest moments of my life: he sat

down beside me, opened his laptop, and—just like in the movies—Cecil began to sweat. His forehead beaded immediately with it. I had always thought this physical response to being caught was the device of lazy writers. Turns out, it happens. His hands, also, shook as he typed in the user name and password.

The inbox revealed a pretty staggering trove of deceit: not only provocative emails between him and the coworker (in her sexy Halloween costume, garter belt and all) but also dozens of emails from "adult" social networking sites. He swore up and down he hadn't met with any of the strangers from online—that he'd only video chatted with some, received a few explicit pictures and posted his own explicit pictures that he took in our bedroom. If you're ever curious what feebleness is, by the way, it's a series of images of a grown man tugging on his penis over dirty white briefs while conspicuously grappling with his laptop's webcam to capture the most alluring angle. I'm still incapable of understanding how one takes oneself seriously while adding a sepia filter.

Not only were there pictures, but the email exchanges were similarly shocking. They'd all begin with a sparkling physical description of himself (height, weight, eye and hair color) and then they'd launch into desperately sad self-promotion. How he enjoyed reading philosophy, how his favorite authors were Hemingway and Fitzgerald, how the music he was currently into was all meticulously sourced, as if he'd gone straight to some online arbiter of cool and listed all the bands reviewed favorably that week. He name-checked half a dozen, just as many authors, all the television shows he liked that were "important" in a cultural sense. In a monumental lack of irony, he listed Plato's *Republic* as one of his favorite books. If I hadn't been so furious, I would have been heartbroken for him: Cecil, distant and anguished by his own feelings of inadequacy wasn't just scavenging the Internet for sex . . . he was also looking for someone to be impressed by him, to find him interesting.

Though fury did come first, my second response was a bizarrely lucid relief that we finally had a legitimate reason to end our foundering relationship. My third was shame—that I could never tell my friends or parents because they'd think less of him and, in turn, think less of me for being with a bad, weak man. Next there was the panic that I'd driven him to cheat on me and it was my fault. He filled a duffel bag and went to stay at a friend's house.

Unfortunately, we were both poor and neither of us could afford to move without the other, much less swallow the penalty of breaking our lease. We were forced to live out the rest of the year (a crushing six months) in our cramped apartment— I in the bedroom and him on the couch. The next half-year was bewildering and isolating: sometimes I missed the way things had been and wanted to forgive him, mostly the sight of him just made me sick. Our closest friends knew what had happened, but we largely masqueraded as a couple in public because the situation was so horrifying that adding a social dimension—pity, even—seemed unbearable.

On the day we moved out of the apartment, I sat on our stoop and watched him walk the long length of the street, ambling into the sunshine with his arms full of boxes. The first few years we were together, we always parted ways with a sweetly embarrassing series of pauses and waves and glances

NIGHT TERRORS | 233

back. This time he didn't look back and I wondered if it was intentionally symbolic or he was just ashamed.

Adjusting to life without him took exactly one week of suffocating depression, insomnia and loss of appetite. Then it was over. It was as if I sweated him out in a fever while unable to sleep at four in the morning and on the eighth day I got up and didn't cry about it ever again. Even though we'd spent (by then) almost four years together, the relationship had died a long time before.

It's impossible to say that I felt any one way about being cheated on. It was all a kind of nausea, moods and sorrows sloshing together: self-loathing, sanctimony, anguish, outrage, relief and a bizarre satisfaction in the confirming of my suspicion he was so flawed. There were also the more literal but no less troubling realizations: that people you love can turn out to be radically different than you thought; that people will lie if it suits them; that they can justify their behaviors even if they know they're awful. But perhaps what hurts the most is that he had to go and do it all with the sort of woman who wears a sexy Halloween costume. Not even a good one, like Sexy Heidegger.

As for Maude, she should hope that two people never have the same dreadful convenience of morality when it comes to her. Our exchange in the office predated my own experience with infidelity, so I'm glad my instincts were on point. If anything, I only gained a more acute understanding of why behavior like this is bad: if you want to ransack someone's self-worth and make that person feel betrayed in one of the most savagely intimate ways, cheat. Or, if you're unhappy in your relationship, end it. In neither scenario exists a place for terminally serious vanity shots of you squeezing your own dick.

I wish there was a better way to say why cheating is bad; that it hurts people is neither a good argument nor a compelling weak one. However, when resorting to deceit and secrecy to satisfy selfish desires at a discernible cost to the well-being of others, it's hard to claim what we're doing is any good. We do something bad, generally, whenever we have to silence the part of us that can instinctively distinguish it from good (unless we are sociopaths, informally diagnosed or otherwise). Honesty is not a virtue in and of itself—as I learned from my effusively direct first boyfriend—and perhaps that's the case because honesty is nothing more than a requirement. Like good hair. And hating Aerosmith.

I'm reminded again of that original anecdote, of my friend saying that human sexuality exists outside the bounds of morality (which also reminds me of how quick I was to dismiss that anecdote as irrelevant to this story, so I guess that was pretty premature). I don't have the authority to decide if things are ultimately moral or not, which may have been where he was going. But I can try to operate from a basic moral premise: that having sex in a "good" way means sex without duplicity, without treachery and especially without sepia-toned peen. Though the ultimately self-serving allusions to Plato can stay.

A FEW THINGS THAT ARE BAD ABOUT SEX

Sometimes I think the world would be better off if we were all just forced to wear signs advertising what we want or are curious about and then we wouldn't have to shit all over other people to get what we're after. For example, if an edgy-looking girl at the bar with tattoos of cassette tapes and scissors and other indie insignia wore a sign that said GIVES HEAD LIKE A BOA CONSTRICTOR BUT FUCKS LIKE A MIME, guys with corresponding interests could simply line up and present their own signs like INTO WEIRD STUFF BUT I'LL CALL YOU AGAIN; TWO MINUTES OF SPORT FUCKING, THEN I GET ANNOYED WITH YOU; WANT TO DRESS UP LIKE A BABY BECAUSE IT'S THE ONLY TIME I FEEL WHOLE and so on. This would save everyone lots of time and energy and potentially debilitating complexes.

No, instead we have to advertise and smell nice and say

the right things and try to demonstrate in myriad ways that we're worth fucking. Unsurprisingly, this can make people really neurotic and self-loathing because they don't believe they're good enough and don't believe anyone will love them. Or want to have sex with them. Even worse, when everyone's neurotic and self-loathing, people tend not to be very hospitable to each other.

We've all been convinced from birth we're not good enough, unless we were overencouraged as children which is arguably worse (seriously—do you want the person performing open heart surgery on you to have gotten a medical degree because he *tried his best*?) and, in response, we urgently attempt to look better and make everyone else look worse. Sometimes this comes from insecurity, sometimes it's a learned behavior, sometimes people are just dicks. The fact of the matter is it's stressing everyone out.

A lot of times, people want to make others feel bad because they feel bad about their own sexual proclivities. As much as politicians would like us to believe that the only kind of sex they have is plodding sober missionary with their spouses while the lights are off, few people are actually so vanilla. If, for example, you like something as pedestrian as a thumb in your ass while receiving oral sex but you're ashamed to ask for that, you might lash out at people who are a little more forthright with their own interests and desires.

Cruel forms of competition are the downside to having a huge dating pool (which is to say, humanity) because people are all too happy to disparage others to make themselves look better in the name of finding a partner. The way we compete is often informed by our sense of shame, our own baggage:

throughout my life I have heard countless women describe other women as sluts and whores, while as many men I've heard describe other men as pussies and faggots. Decent, thoughtful people don't talk this way, possibly because they're decent and thoughtful, possibly because they're not afraid to ask for a thumb in their ass and don't go around resenting other people because they're just really satisfied all the time.

Think about all the hours in your life you've wasted dieting or matching your socks or thinking your nose isn't straight enough or worried people will notice that blue vein on your leg or concerned your vagina tastes like old movie nachos. We adorn ourselves with interesting clothing, we accessorize, we take showers and try to have good posture and listen to the right records and say perceptive things about the movies we're supposed to like. We remove our pubic hair or we don't or we discuss it in extremely cryptic noncommittal ways without ever really confirming whether we have it or not because using humor and *Jurassic Park* to obfuscate unease brings us back to what I'm talking about: shame, insecurity and self-loathing as they often manifest in shitting on other people and making the world worse.

Men and women compete in very different ways. Well, actually, both men and women are pretty quick to say awful things about perceived rivals, real or straw. Men and women also have similar sets of insecurities, toxic body image and terrible tattoo decision-making abilities. It's the actual physical manifestation of those insecurities that's different. Well, no. Mostly men just go to the gym and women eat salad or they eat steak and brag about it.

Men have it really rough. They've been conditioned to believe they all have to be cowboys and lone wolves and construction workers and should be ashamed if they become flight attendants or nurses or actuaries. They're told they need to have these triangle-shaped torsos and square jaws and spend all day in the gym or chopping wood until they develop thighs that can crush two-liter soda bottles (it's nebulous how, though) and, more than anything, they have to be really potent. I mean semen-wise.

This is the most critically important aspect of the "what it takes to be a man" rubric: potency. No woman wants a guy who's shooting blanks because the secret of masculinity exists in ribbons of seminal fluid somewhere deep within and if semen doesn't have masculinity inside then it's no different from the slime trails that snails leave and if humans aren't more noble than snails, then what of art? What's especially sad about this ideal of the hyperpotent male is that it's totally true and nonnegotiable. I think it's because there's no hiding one's impotency? You can always tell when a sterile man comes inside you. It's like a dog whistle.

Women have it even more rough because they get old and become invisible the second they can't pass for "just turned eighteen like a month ago" anymore. If you're a woman, you have a pretty short shelf life and then you have to start spewing out babies so people will know you're not brittle. You also can't go too far with being attractive, otherwise you invite rape and everyone will think you're shallow. Moreover, as terrifying as it sounds that people might think you're shallow if you wear lipstick, rape is a serious problem. It actually makes it quite hard for chaste women to live in big cities. I mean, obviously, it's not a huge problem for promiscuous women, but for women who care about their honor and don't wear makeup, rape is a constant fear. I'm personally not afraid of being raped because, in addition to my solitary nature, every time I go into a scary neighborhood at night I just put my hair up in a really unflattering ponytail.

Competition naturally makes people a little more aggressive and self-serving, but when it's compounded by shame or insecurity, it gets vicious. This manifests in unintelligent people as, for example, women calling other women fat, men calling other men pussies, homophobes hating gays or the transgendered or anything but the aforementioned sober missionary sex with the lights off. Because as far as the deeply stupid are concerned, the worst thing you can be as a woman is not thin and the worst thing you can be as a man is feminine and they all agree that the worst thing you can be is anything other than very straight (and toned and wealthy, etc.). All that vileness and hate comes from deep fears of inadequacy and if that isn't confirmation of an almost primordial lack of intellect, then you're a fat pussy faggot. Luckily, we are not chiefly concerned with the wants of the deeply stupid.

Unluckily, many more problems result from the pride and obliviousness of the half-smart, like myself. So I would like to explain how shame and insecurity and subsequent ruthless competitiveness made me really shitty as a person: I spent a lot of my life sensitive to this idea that being a woman is terrible.

As a young girl, you're bombarded by ideas and images that are supposed to make you feel bad about yourself (so you'll buy this expensive horseshit that promises to plump your lips or that useless strip of tape that supposedly removes skin "impurities"). I internalized it all and then decided I was different and that this kind of stuff was targeted at other women, women who "nagged," women who squealed at spiders, women who counted every calorie, women who had little yappy dogs they carried around in purses with stupid designer logos splashed across the side. All that was for them. Not me. I was different.

Which was just as well, because I never saw myself fitting into girl culture and I regarded its products—those magazines, chick flicks, books with lipstick kisses on the cover—as grim totems from another world. I also became a tomboy very naturally, through a combination of my towering height (always in the back of every class photo) and proximity (all the kids on my block were boys). From the moment, at age ten, when I first wrapped a clod of grass into an empty crayon wrapper and taped it shut and tried to smoke it to impress my male next-door neighbor, I was effectively edged out of the world of pretty princesses and into cool unisex shit like vandalism and alchemy. Years of baggy rock T-shirts and ill-fitting men's jeans followed.

My identity as a tomboy was consistently reinforced and rewarded once junior high came around: other girls appeared jealous of the nonsexual attention I received from boys. Soon, I came to believe that having mostly male friends made me better. I'm not entirely sure how this certainty dominated my teen years so much; it had something to do with shame and disappointment at being a girl, though the actual sociological reasons behind this are a little too convoluted for me to chase after here. I'm sure I'd have a much greater understanding of that now had I been a women's studies major, but I figure if you're going to go into suffocating debt for a college education, you might as well learn something.

Growing up, you encounter a lot of those callow girls who claim to have cool boy interests and go around saying provocative things like "I'm a misogynist" and "I don't have female friends" and that women's studies joke up there. What's weird about that phenomenon is girls who go around boasting about how they have no female friends want you to think it's because they have these robustly masculine brains and are too reasonable for the world of lady pettiness and are just super interesting and cool on almost manlike levels, but these women don't realize they're just advertising the fact that they're cunts. Trying to distinguish yourself from other stupid women is just another strategy to seem more fuckable and, insofar as you are cultivating a persona to be more fuckable, you are engaged in the activity of every stupid, venal, petty, shallow, purse dog–toting woman in history from whom you are supposedly trying to distinguish yourself. This person was me.

By the time I got to college, my slowly cultivated isolation from my own gender was at the forefront of my ideas about myself; I proudly announced to anyone seemingly interested that I was a misogynist and a lot of men would hear that and nod really approvingly, as if to say, "Finally, a woman I can hate women with." I thought this not only made me seem appealing because I was provocative and would say provocative things, but because I was trying to affect traditionally masculine qualities, like reasonableness and being annoyed by cupcakes and not watching romantic comedies. The irony lost on me, though, was that if you're a woman congratulating yourself for being masculine, you are indeed participating in misogyny . . . by being the victim of it. Which totally defeats the purpose.

Many women are instructed to see other women as rivals who can't be trusted. However, one really unexpected twist of this social conditioning is others regard it as further reason to find women terrible: we talk about disagreements between women as catfights; we dismiss criticisms that women have of other women as symptoms of primitive envy; we view female friendship as a strategic, frivolous, volatile thing.

Interestingly, women are capable of disliking each other for reasons other than superficiality and pettiness. Yes, every now and again a woman can be unlikeable for lack of intellect and integrity, and—miraculously—other women are able to claw themselves from their morass of vaginal jealousy, neurosis and poor self-esteem to recognize that. They can actually recognize that another woman sucks because she just does. For example, my ex-boyfriend's new girlfriend is an idiot. This has nothing to do with feelings of inferiority or perceived competition; she's actually an untalented moron. This should be totally fine to acknowledge—because she's so terrible that it's impossible not to—but she *is* thinner than me, which weakens my case. That's why I've been on a diet; once I lose ten pounds, my derision for her is going to be completely unbiased.

Even though I'm able to say she's insufferable, I can still admit I've wasted a lot of my life cutting down others, especially women, to make myself feel better or appear more attractive. As a painfully awkward, insecure teenager uncomfortable with my female physiognomy, I dealt with my shame by blaming it on other women. Of course you're going to resent good-looking, well-dressed, nice, hygienic ladies if you've spent most of your formative years worried your vagina smells like a duck pond. Or wet popcorn. Or a retirement center. Or gumbo seasoning.

It all changed when one day, at a bar surrounded by male friends and after a lifetime of boasting that I had no female ones, someone made casual reference to this ("Well, Ashley, you don't have any female friends"). Much to my surprise, I corrected him and explained that many of my oldest and most intimate friendships were with women, which was true. Although I'd always positioned myself as someone without female friends, the moment I heard someone say it back, it repulsed me. I insisted that my female friends were smart and interesting and funny (and shorter than me, mercifully) and that's when I stopped pretending they didn't exist to make men like me more.

This is also when I kind of realized that everyone just needs to calm down and stop fretting that they're not enough. There's no point in pretending to be something you're not, or throwing your female friends under the bus, or abusing your body to correspond to the tastes of some abstract person, or doing anything false because you want potential partners to view you as very special. When you calm down, someone will love you . . . because you're not horrible. They'll love you and your blue veins and your wonky eyebrow and your gross feet and your probably very normal-smelling genitals.

———

O r, you could just keep chugging along, being terrible. The only problem with that is if everyone sits back and becomes content with being shitty then we end up with a shitty world. Imagine that, a world where no one tried to be good: everyone has little yappy dogs they don't pick up after, bread is always stale, no one ever dunks a basketball or opens doors for anyone else, Michael Jackson would never have moonwalked (or made *Off the Wall!*), while all songs are about how hard it is to be famous and we listen to them on Zunes.

Unfortunately, telling people not to be shitty is kind of the problem, too. To my mind the solution is this: better oneself where possible, but don't marginalize others for failing to do the same. That's it. Try especially hard not to shame or judge people for their sexual proclivities even though adult babies are still extremely unsettling and I don't know if I can get past it because I'm just not a saint.

Then again, sex has become so overemphasized that maybe the only way we'll improve as a species is if we all agree to put a moratorium on fucking and go off and read books and learn important shit and know about history and stop looking at people blankly when politics come up and maybe cultivate some actual ideas about our lives and go to museums and refrain from taking cell phone pictures of the art. Maybe then people will start having legitimate thoughts and will create stuff and then everyone will actually be better and smarter and we'll be just like the ancient Greeks, who never had sex under any circumstances and just sat around thinking important thoughts and that's why they went extinct, which is what *The Iliad* is about.

It's not completely our fault. Sex is everywhere and

unavoidable—from the moment we hit puberty (or a little before, thanks to those fucked up dreams about Prince I kept
having) we start assembling a collection of facts of what we
think we know about sex. We learn about sex from strangers,
who never have our best interests in mind (hence the appeal of
"fucking in Paris"). We learn about sex from our peers (hence
"shitting out your vagina"). We learn about sex from the the
Internet (hence "SpaghettiOs"). We learn about sex from candlelit love scenes in movies, from casual violence in mainstream
porn, from hundreds of hours reading racy fan fiction on the
Internet about Wolverine and Jean Grey and their passionate
forbidden love—and all of those sources offer wildly different,
variously unrealistic ideas about sex itself. We're so inundated
with the idea of sex's all-consuming importance that a lot of
people care more about just having it than making it good.
This probably has something to do with why sex makes us so
awful sometimes, which in turn leads to people having so
much shame about it.

I had a friend who worked in a porn shop outside Chicago for
a few years. By "shop," I really mean porn Walmart: a lone
concrete fortress along a highway, a self-sustaining strip mall
hunched over the asphalt, inviting perverts, weirdos and regular people who hadn't figured out the Internet in its lawless
early days. My friend—we'll call him Henry—worked there
five days a week and so pretty quickly became acquainted with
the shop's regulars. It had never really occurred to me that
porn shops have regulars the way bars or restaurants do but
it's exactly the same. There were all kinds, having manifold
kinks and social tics and skin conditions. One smelled over-

poweringly of broccoli and rented titles only from the Dirty Debutantes series. Another was a handsome, clean-cut corporate lawyer exclusively interested in water sports. Another would rent a stack of a dozen titles in the morning and bring them all back that afternoon. Part of Henry's job was disinfecting the DVD cases.

The regular who most fascinates me was also the most mundane of the bunch: plain-faced, middle-aged, just beginning to bald, no style to speak of, average height. He was an unremarkable man in every way, the sort of person whom you have to occasionally be reminded of even if you're talking to him. He was also one of the most polite customers; he kept to himself, never caused any trouble, never acted weird. Every single week, without fail, he would come in on Wednesday around eight p.m. and spend an hour in the store, walking through the aisles. He would often appear to be agonizing over what to rent, shuffling back and forth through different sections, placing a hand to his chin thoughtfully while he stood in front of walls of gang-bang videos and spring break narratives. The minutes would tick by and closing time would loom and his agitation would increase.

Then, every single Wednesday, an hour or two after he arrived and right before closing, the Regular would come up to the front desk with a stack of five to eight titles (porn shop patrons seldom rent just one, I've also learned) and put them on the counter. Every Wednesday, the man would set down his DVDs and they would all be the same thing: chicks with dicks. *Shemale Fiesta* stuff.

The highlight of Henry's day, however, would come when this mild-mannered patron set down the DVDs, casually leaned on the counter and looked at him sideways, affecting a pained air of casual cool.

Then, every Wednesday, the Regular would say, "Yeee-up. Tryin' somethin' new this week."

The first time it happened, Henry wanted to shrug and explain that people rented far weirder titles all the time, but he refrained. The third or fourth time it happened, Henry thought the Regular was joking. By the time Henry was approaching two years of employment at this enormous porn complex, he realized the Regular liked only shemale porn and was extremely embarrassed by it.

In addition to being fascinated by someone who (seemingly) got off to one thing only, I was pretty saddened by this story. No one should have to go through life, Wednesday in and Wednesday out, being embarrassed by liking what he likes. Nobody should have to live out his whole existence thinking there's something really awful about what turns him on, especially when the fact is there's just nothing wrong with an adult male wanting to watch adult trans-women with male genitalia fuck each other. Frankly, a lifetime of nothing but sober missionary in the dark is more fetishistic.

There are a lot of ways to have healthy, fun, uninhibited, great sex with someone—too many for anyone to go around feeling embarrassed about what gets him or her off. Though the easiest approach is probably solid communication and some chemistry, everything else is completely unique to the people having it and no one will ever learn anything meaningful about sex from stupid silly books about sex (especially ones where sex is conspicuously absent).

In other words: be madly in love in a monogamous relationship or have sex with dozens of strangers—have whatever kind of sex you want with adults who want to have sex with you—*just don't be dark about it.* Don't cheat; don't lie; don't shame people. Don't do anything you don't want to do, don't stifle your own enjoyment for the sake of someone else and be safe. And have empathy and compassion. Which is a pretty earnest message, considering all those abortion jokes I made earlier.

Besides, maybe those videos were really wholesome too, like the shemales were Red Cross nurses aiding hurricane disaster victims with the help of their secret penises and rations. You don't know.

BREEDING

I definitely want to have kids. Unfortunately, you can't be middle class and college educated without a swell of guilt whenever you consider breeding. You also can't ever, under any circumstances, complain about being middle class and college educated, or things pertaining to it.

Up until about age twenty-one, I hated babies. I'd see them at playgrounds, appendages sagging helplessly through legholes in swings. In their finery. I developed a reputation among friends for being rude to babies at neighboring tables in restaurants. When I was a teenager, I was at a Chinese restaurant with my father and going on about how a nearby baby looked like Winston Churchill, melting. The baby's steward (presumably dad) stood up in an act of intimidation and my father had to smooth things over. Another time, I was at a chain steakhouse in a roadside strip mall in the desert surrounding Albuquerque and I saw this one baby: the back of its head was flat enough to roll out a pie crust. I learned later that this is usually caused by parental negligence and babies with flat heads have to wear corrective helmets so they can enter adulthood with normal, human-shaped heads. I knew another baby once, he had a ball pit.

Babies, if you consider it, are good at one thing: becoming adults. Which isn't that impressive, honestly. If you or I were given eighteen years to perform a single task, we'd probably succeed. If not, we'd be no better than infants. Besides simply getting older, they're also able to run around naked with aplomb, they have weird undeveloped little bodies and they carry a sling of their own excrement wherever they go. Then, of course, they present legitimate problems, such as overpopulation, deforestation, global warming and refusing to skateboard *even when I put them on the board.*

Moreover, nothing beats the sanctimony of new parents for pure, raging awfulness. Having waited tables for years, I can tell you that new parents are the worst people alive: nowhere but in the mind of a new parent is it acceptable to engage in adult activities (like dining) but bring along a small, fleshy symbol of destruction, one able to shriek for hours on end at frequencies human beings are genetically hardwired to abhor. People would bring their infants to the nice enough restaurant where I worked, and the infants would sit at the table and do nothing but throw food for the entire meal. Then they'd leave, and it never occurred to them once that restaurant staff are only supposed to pick up after guests *within reason.* When you're a busy waiter, nothing breaks your balls worse than having to get down under a table on all fours and pick up Cheerios, fruit snacks and individual corn kernels scattered over an eight-foot radius.

By far the worst thing that I have ever experienced at a restaurant—excepting the two old swingers who would come in and tell me my hands "smelled of oranges" and insist I go to their apartment for Pernod after my shift—occurred while I worked at this Asian fusion place in Maryland. It happened at an outdoor table directly in front of the restaurant, beside a giant window looking onto the dining room. Two young parents finished their meal, moved aside their dishes and changed their baby right there. Right on the table. Where people dine. Immediately beside other people dining. Unsurprisingly, the kinds of assholes who'd change a baby on a table in a crowded dining area are exactly the kind of selfish, awful, entitled, thoughtless people who'd finish, get up and leave the dirty diaper.

Right about age twenty-one, though, something in me turned. I started waving to babies on the street. I started asking people with babies if I could hold them. I started babysitting on weekends so I could hang out with babies, like some weird junkie who needed to be around bad smells and coloring books.

It probably goes without saying that I was never the sort of girl who thought about her wedding. Not that there's anything wrong with that. Well, obviously there kind of is (which is the party line again?). I don't really give a shit about marriage, essentially; I think it's a nice institution and obviously I think everyone should be able to do it if they want. I'm not against it, but I won't seek it out either and I certainly never dreamed about the dress or location or cake or napkin rings or any of the details that would surely drive me insane if I were burdened with caring about them. I guess I regard marriage with the same congenial indifference that I feel toward modern art and classical music and memoirs written by twentysomethings who haven't lived in any discernible interesting way. Having and raising children, however, seems great. If you can sweep the guilt under the rug.

The guilt is immense. It is immeasurable. It is a vast sea of self-loathing at the very thought of bringing another selfish, consumptive monster into a dying world. It's almost like a science fiction story, it's so appalling.

But! If you're neurotic enough to be suffocated under this guilt, you're also probably a pretty shrewd sophist. You work around it by reminding yourself of all the shitty people out there who are breeding with abandon, just spilling babies from their distended guts as they heave back giant sodas during marathons of competition-based reality television. These people don't consider the overwhelming consequences of rapid population growth, of diminishing land, of finite resources. It's our duty, as the reasonable, the decent and the competent, to balance them out.

Since I'm not a respectable baby-having age—well, the modern equivalent of that; I'm actually pretty past my prime in terms of pure biological function—this penultimate story isn't about me. It's also a much, much better story about having children than I'll ever have, unless in a few years I discover my womb is made of hummingbirds able to breathe in blood or something. Obviously that couldn't be topped.

In the grandest tradition of sex stories, this one is about "a friend of a friend," specifically my friend Raymond. Not even, really—more like an acquaintance of Raymond's, which I think is more often subsequently passed off as a friend of a friend story because brevity is the soul of bar jokes. Most of these stories, these testaments to darkness and humiliation wreaking havoc on people we don't know that well, are almost invariably about anal sex going horribly wrong. This one is just about a man and his wife trying to have a baby.

They had a child but wanted another, and after many months of no luck eventually decided to pursue fertility treatments. Raymond's Friend was the overanalytical neurotic type with whom you are abundantly familiar, thanks to the many others that dot the landscape of this book. Raymond's Friend was suffering no small amount of performance anxiety, augmented, it would seem, by the whole giant unfeeling medical apparatus into which he'd entered.

When originally told he would be expected to masturbate into a cup, he was put off by the strange iciness of the vocabulary: his semen in a cup, for one, lost all vestige of intimacy and animalism with the moniker "a sample," which makes sense as a medical euphemism but is no less off-putting for the person to whom it represents progeny, legacy and immortality. Worse still, in one sweeping act to eliminate the human drama from the situation, Raymond's Friend would also be referred to as simply "the person submitting a sample," as opposed to "wisher," "dreamer," "nerve-racked hopeful father" or "masturbator."

Raymond's Friend was beginning to really suffer under

the anxiety of "the act of producing a sample" until he learned that, since he lived within thirty minutes of the fertility clinic, he would actually be able to produce the sample in the comfort of his own home. Raymond's Friend would escape the stark, antiseptic brutality of the fertility clinic's masturbatorium and its folded brittle dirty magazines and shiny rubber tree. He would be free to choose any pornography he wanted.

This unchecked, boundless freedom, of course, is the space where neurotics go to die. A place without limitations, without direction, without guidance, is the place where anxious people like Raymond's Friend and myself and so many others find the metaphorical fetid standing water where nervous breakdowns spawn. This is exactly what happened.

For starters, there were a few small problems. Raymond's Friend was, as mentioned, put off by the clinical speak surrounding the ordeal. Second, apparently, you can't use lubricant because it kills sperm. Third, his wife was upstairs the whole time, contributing to the pressure of producing his sample on demand.

Before we continue, I must pause and say the reason I know this story is because my friend Raymond knew about my book and cheerfully offered the account. I told him I would need a few more details, but Raymond knew the guy only so well. Raymond, heroically, called this man he barely knew and, after chatting with him about the weather, initiated this very intimate conversation. Sadly, our information lacks one glaring detail: why couldn't his wife help? Neither Raymond nor I know, but Raymond's Friend was alone in this struggle to produce a sample. Raymond wasn't about to push and go asking for anything more than was volunteered. We must assume that his wife, too, was put off by the clinical aspects. All we know is that she sat upstairs, waiting.

The real problem was porn. Because you can't just jerk off to any old schoolgirl fantasy or DP scenario. This is the porn that will produce your offspring. These tawdry images will forever be linked to the children you raise and love. If anything, the porn you choose plays as much a role in conceiving your child as you do. The porn has to be special. The porn has to mean something. This is where Raymond's Friend lost his mind.

He tried. With each video or set of images, he couldn't shake the feeling that these globe-breasted, orange-skinned caricatures of femininity, these joyless tattooed mountains of meat and sinew, were participating in *the creation of his child*. He couldn't handle it. A few failed attempts at masturbating later, Raymond's Friend put down his penis and got to thinking.

After much soul searching, Raymond's Friend produced a list of qualifications he would require of the porn he'd use to masturbate his future child into existence. These are they.

> First, the woman depicted must be anonymous. The woman should have a vague, regular face, an unmemorable canvas. He could not use a famous porn star because every time he would come across said porn star in the future, he would be reminded of gazing into her eyes and not his wife's while firing off his semen into a receptacle, again not inside of his wife but in-

stead into the hollow of the cup's cold plastic as it scraped against his glans.

Second, it must be free of perversion, his reasoning being that the father's illicit thoughts at the time of ejaculation might somehow affect the character of his children. He figured he better not chance it. Moreover, when his child is old enough to ask questions about the circumstances of his or her conception, he'd rather not discuss the plot of *Homey in the Haystack*, wherein a city slicker witnesses a crime and enters the witness protection program and is sent off to live with the Amish, which is uneventful until one of the wholesome Amish daughters spies him pissing in a field and is impressed by the enormity of his cock, such that, one by one, they all remove their clothes (and reveal their clit piercings and pubic tats) and he systematically nails the many Amish daughters. That wouldn't do at all. He's got to select something with at least a vague moral quality.

Third: timelessness. In our memory of events, we recall mostly our feelings, while our more regrettable hairstyles go largely unrecorded, our chokers and stirrup pants and boot cut jeans go unobserved. Until, of course, we see pictures of our past and this is all that stands out. Because Raymond's Friend found himself in the unique, if not extraordinary, position to have a photographic record of perhaps the most monumental act of his life . . . he'd prefer it to be high quality and not dated. Obviously he had no intention of ever memorializing this image, but if or when he ever crossed it again, he'd prefer it not to scream "early 2010s" or "even the porn stars were wearing those stupid high-waisted pants" or "your fixation on the search term 'embarrassed Latina' is now, in turn, deeply embarrassing to you."

Fourth, and this is the surprise: a maternal aspect. Some part of the stimuli should include a visual prompt or reminder that he is procreating. Ninety-nine-point-nine percent of all the ejaculations in his life are for his own pleasure and this time his ejaculation will count, will actually achieve its biological aim, so the pornography should include some recognition of that.

So what did Raymond's Friend eventually settle upon to produce his future child? What image or footage included anonymity, some discernible purity, timelessness and a respectful nod to the role of motherhood?

It was simple: a naked woman in a bathtub full of milk. The milk was deep and opaque (as bathtubs full of it are wont) such that the only visible nudity was her breasts, rising from the surface, dairy beading across her abdomen. It was a PG-13 image that objectified the anonymous woman into nothing more than a free-floating head and bobbing breasts. She looked into the camera and licked her lips coquettishly. She had a timeless, pinup-quality face that was at once feminine and ordinary, a face that says, "This is what you want, isn't it? Now, hurry up."

Sure enough, Raymond's Friend's child and his or her

many unborn brethren splattered into that little plastic cup. When he finished, he figured he must conceal the sample somehow, for civility's sake, and set about looking for a brown paper bag. Unfortunately, once his seed had spilled, the unseen timer began and he had only thirty minutes to get to the clinic, a fifteen-minute drive away. His search for the brown paper bag became frantic until he was left with no choice but to unsheath a half-eaten cheeseburger and use a day-old McDonald's Happy Meal container. Raymond's Friend, having lost no small amount of valuable travel time to searching for a brown paper bag, was forced to carry "the sample" in a heavily branded and already dehumanizing reminder of his own feebleness. With it, he dove into his car and started for the clinic.

Raymond's Friend had also been instructed to keep the sample warm. Inevitably, there was traffic. While sitting on the highway, he glanced over at the Happy Meal box full of his own semen and, worried, turned on the chair's electric heater. Unsatisfied still with the sample (with his progeny!) alone and far away on that slowly warming chair, Raymond's Friend did what any man would do: he reached over, picked it up and nestled it between his legs like a mother hen. For good measure, he then turned on the heat of the driver's seat.

Finally, Raymond's Friend arrived at the fertility clinic toting his McDonald's bag full of semen and walked through the waiting room full of grinning idiots who knew full well what was in his hands. Raymond's Friend and his wife eventually had a beautiful daughter.

You might think this story is about how neurotic types need structure or else their crazy brains will eat themselves.

That's true. You might also think this story is a testament to the neurotic's ability to solve problems with nuance and thoughtfulness. That's true, too. Further, you might think this story is about how a Happy Meal box has more uses than carrying fast food. Obviously true, but this story is mostly about how every birth is a miracle.

ONE TIME, I HAD SEX

A lot of popular writing about sex can be boiled down to "I fucked some people. I didn't learn anything. Thanks to my casual use of the f-word, you know I'm being candid." And what's fucked up about that is a lot of purveyors of this material think that, by virtue of announcing their flaws and insecurities and hang-ups and unchecked selfishness, they're completely absolved of doing anything about it. Not that one should look to sex writing for a moral compass, but if you're a shitty person, the most likely reason you're shitty is you don't care about being better.

This is a roundabout way of saying that I could justify writing this insofar as it's not actually about me having sex— it's more about anxiety and morality and alienation and absurdity and the whole mental morass of sex and some people I have known. There's no way I could write about myself actually having sex, because that shit is cheap like casual swears.

Unless you can actually bring new insight to the act itself (like you're a contortionist or something), your own sex life is best left in fiction. This paragraph is another way of saying I'm special.

So, why write about sex and never talk about actually having it?

For one, I'm a coward. If women talk about actually having sex, it makes them sluts. If women accept or own people calling them sluts, it confirms they're sluts. If they complain about being called sluts, they're antifeminist. If they complain about being called sluts because they object to the loaded, antifemale sentiment of that term, they're militant feminists (the least fuckable kind). If you've suddenly embroiled yourself in a conversation about how being a woman affects why people are criticizing you, you have lost. And you've lost half your audience.

Books about men having sex are about not just sex but also life, mortality and humanity. Books about women having sex are for women. If this book were just for women, you'd know because there would be a lipstick kiss, cupcake or champagne bottle in the foreground of the cover and a Manhattan skyline in the back. The typeface would be cursive in order to appear as though I'd scrawled it myself in a hurry while dashing off to some aspirational department store for an afternoon of conspicuous consumption. Nope. Cats tossing salad.

Another huge objection I have to writing about the sex I've had is selling out the people I've had it with. I see these books sometimes, written by people my age, who thinly veil their subjects (or don't even bother) and then ruthlessly parse their sexual dysfunctions. Although everything you've read here actually happened (especially the bird guy), I've done a pretty meticulous job of obscuring the identities of those who would object. To their credit, the people in question accepted being written about with compassion, encouragement and dignity.

I never made much of a traditional sex writer because (1) I don't want to talk about my own sex life and (2) I don't have that much material. I've never even had a one-night stand or anything that might be considered casual. I can assure you that it's not because of anyone oppressing me. Another reason I don't write about my sex life is I'm just not very good in bed. Honestly. I'm not anywhere near thin enough to be that unremarkable at something and still get away with doing it.

But, in order to avoid sounding like I'm just congratulating myself for being special, I'll tell you why this book isn't about my sex life. And that story happens to be about one time I had sex.

One night, during my freshman year of college, there was a big party in an outdoor common area. Everyone was congregating and drinking and I was with my friends Matt and Dave. I was dating the Mormon at the time. The reason I don't have a problem with talking frankly about the Mormon in this book is because he was fundamentally a decent guy and absolutely fantastic in bed, so even though we were comically ill-suited to each other, I can still say nice things about him. He could even use this book like a sexual résumé—maybe after he blocks out the part where he took me to see the bishop? Maybe he'll meet a girl who's into that.

Anyway, the Mormon and I left the party early. Our friends Matt and Dave made a crack about how we were prob-

ably going to go have sex. We laughed it off and then confirmed their suspicions by going back to his room—the
window of which overlooked this outdoor area—and not turning on the lights.

The Mormon's room was what we called a "dumbbell
double," two rooms with one door, and about three-quarters
of a wall between them. There wasn't much privacy in the
dorm, but we should have been studying anyway, so this was
our own fault. What's more, the Mormon's roommate was an
unhinged celibate Christian Scientist libertarian and wasn't in
the room that night, probably off in space not giving medicine
to children. For a couple reasons.

This meant, of course, that the Mormon and I were free
to fool around. Which was great because he was so good at it.
If you're reading this right now, Mormon Parents, you should
be proud. Sex with him was the kind that can make a person
believe in God. He was practically a missionary.

So we were having sex but we had to leave the door unlocked for his insane celibate Christian Scientist libertarian
roommate, who I guess never remembered his keys because of
Milton Friedman or something, and so the Mormon almost
always left the door unlocked. You'd think his roommate
would reject that kind of thing as charity. But that would be
an inconvenience.

The Mormon and I hadn't really started things yet and
we were covered with blankets, so when the door opened, we
weren't even terribly startled. Matt and Dave, drunk out of
their minds, stumbled into the room and pointed at the bed.

"You guysss," one of them slurred, "why aren't you downstairs? Having fun?"

"Yeah!" agreed the other.

"Go away," we said.

"No," they said and Matt turned around, pulled down his pants and mooned us. Dave followed suit.

"Get out of here," we said, exasperated.

"You guys are fucking lame," they said and pulled up their pants and wandered off.

The Mormon and I went back to what we were doing. We did not get up and lock the door, again in deference to his emotionally unhinged celibate Christian Scientist libertarian roommate.

About twenty minutes went by and Dave and Matt stumbled back into the room. Matt had his pants half off by the time he'd come through the door. He turned and pulled down his boxers and mooned us again. Dave, smaller, got his pants to about his shins and turned but in so doing tripped on Matt and fell into the wall adjoining the rooms. He somehow managed to take Matt down with him. Suddenly there were two boys with their butts out, writhing around in confusion and laughing at the mouth of the dorm, door still wide open onto the hallway. Thankfully, again, there was a blanket over us.

"You guy have the hairiest asses I've ever seen," the Mormon said.

"Fuck you!" they yelled. They scrambled up on their feet and charged the bed. Dave was the first to land on top, pinning the Mormon and effectively pinning me. Not to be outdone, Matt plunged onto the bed and on top of Dave, squishing all of us into one big, homoerotic pile.

It should go without saying that neither Matt nor Dave had bothered to get their pants back on, and so they writhed around on top of us, making high-pitched cooing noises and saying things like, "Oooh, we're having sex," and rotating and grinding through the blankets. Neither myself nor the Mormon had yelled any objections to this invasion and therefore the boys hadn't gotten the shock and horror they were after. The cooing and grinding went on for another minute until an eerie clarity pervaded their mischief. The room went silent.

"Guys," I said and it was the only time I ever nailed a deadpan that mattered, "he's inside of me right now."

They squealed like frightened babies, springing backward and yanking their jeans up in a fluid motion. They fell on top of each other again on the way out and screamed at that and then ran screaming down the hallway until they reached the bottom floor of the dorm and burst outside and we could hear their screams in the night through the open window. The Mormon and I carried on, unperturbed, and then went to sleep.

I tell this story now, at the end of this book that's my sex memoir but not about my sex life, because it's a pretty perfect distillation of what I was going for. Sure it was infantile and absurd, but there was a concrete lesson to be learned: no one wants to hear about me having sex. You have to be receptive to feedback.

ACKNOWLEDGMENTS

I must first address my father and brother, both of whom have extraordinary senses of humor. Thank you for shaping mine.

Thanks to my wonderful agent, Erin Malone, and everyone at WME.

Thanks to Patrick Mulligan for buying this thing. Thanks to Lauren Marino for believing in it. Thanks to Emily Wunderlich, indefatigable and brimming with compassion—you are the foil every author needs.

To the now-defunct B5 Media, thanks for being the first people to pay for my writing and welcoming me to republish some of that material in this very book.

Special thanks to . . .

Jennifer Wright, for giving me my break.

Lauren Leto, who stuck her neck out for me.

A few friends who were kind enough to offer invaluable

feedback (and patience) throughout this process: Nic Rad, Liana Maeby, Patrick Moberg, Erica Gorochow, Dylan Parry, Ann Talley, Emily Andrews, Ranjan Das.

Thanks to Matt Langer for being my friend for like 1,000 years.

Thanks to Karen McCann for knowing more about this than me and always making herself available.

Thanks to David Gluck, who I called immediately when I found out I'd sold my first book and who said simply, "Don't fuck this up." I can't express how fortunate I was to get so much of his time and how grateful I am to see his influence all over this book. Dave, few people ever get a friend like you.

To Jeremy Schoenherr, for everything.

Strangely and unexpectedly, most of all: enormous gratitude to my dear friend Ben Lansky, who one day a few years ago in a yellowing stairwell was the first person to ever tell me I was funny. It surprised me at the time but I gave it a shot.

ABOUT THE AUTHOR

Jeremy Hunt Schoenherr

Ashley Cardiff grew up in Northern California. She studied classics at St. John's College. She lives in Brooklyn.